JonBenet Ramsey: Prostitution of Justice

Doc Miller

Photographs by Judith Z. Phillips

Copyright © 2026 Doc Miller

Paperback ISBN: 979-8-218-94585-5
Hardcover ISBN: 979-8-218-94584-8
eBook ISBN: 979-8-218-94586-2

All rights reserved. Any unauthorized reprint or use of this material is strictly prohibited. No part of this book may be reproduced or transmitted in any form or by any means, electronic or mechanical, including photocopying, recording, or by any information storage and retrieval system without express written permission from the author.

All reasonable attempts have been made to verify the accuracy of the information provided in this publication. Nevertheless, the author assumes no responsibility for any errors and/or omissions.

2026

Dedication

For Judith and JonBenet and for my sons, Justin and Trey

Table of Contents

Part One: Crime of the Century - 1

Chapter One: Depravity, Handled Deftly - 3

Chapter Two: Contamination - 10

Chapter Three: Credible Millionaires - 18

Chapter Four: Quandaries - 28

Chapter Five: The Gold Rush - 37

Chapter Six: "We Know Who You Are" - 47

Chapter Seven: A Legendary Theory - 57

Chapter Eight: Invisible Evidence - 71

Chapter Nine: Real News Fake NEWS - 83

Chapter Ten: We Did It - 98

Part Two: The JonBenet Ramsey Murder - 103

Chapter One: The Curse - 105

Chapter Two: Crimes and Punishments - 117

Chapter Three: Tabloid Man - 135

Chapter Four: Tales from the Macabre - 145

Chapter Five: Rent - 166

Chapter Six: Information Brokers - 175

Chapter Seven: The Impresario of Pasta - 186

Part Three: Reasonable Doubt for a Reasonable Fee - 198

Chapter One: Taking Out Snakes - 200

Chapter Two: Mountains Like Pyramids - 209

Chapter Three: Yee Olde Grand Jury - 222

Chapter Four: Operation Desert Glow - 233

Chapter Five: A Witch's Potion - 251

Chapter Six: The Wizards of Laws - 261

Chapter Seven: Aftermath - 271

On October 25, 2013, Boulder Judge J. Robert Lowenbach released to the public grand jury transcripts from 1999 in which John and Patsy Ramsey were indicted for child abuse resulting in death and for assisting a person for the crime of murder in the first degree. The foreman of the grand jury signed the true bill. The story of the indictment lies somewhere within the millions of hits the phrase "JonBenet Ramsey" receives on the internet. The unsigned indictment and the gagged jurors remain inexplicably unimportant.

Boulder District Attorney, Alex Hunter, after announcing the grand jury "decision" claimed in a nationally televised interview, "We do not have sufficient evidence to warrant the filing of charges." This is the true story of the manipulation of the criminal justice system in Colorado that denied justice in the murder of JonBenet Ramsey.

Prostitution of Justice

Part One:

Crime of the Century

Boulder Creek – Boulder, Colorado

Prostitution of Justice

Prostitution of Justice

Chapter One: Depravity, Handled Deftly

The masquerade began at 5:52 a.m. on December 26, 1996. "We have a kidnapping! Hurry please!" Patsy Ramsey cried to the 911 operator. By then, as the autopsy report has since revealed, JonBenet Ramsey already lay dead as rigor mortis set in, stiffening her muscles and freezing her limbs within death's grip. Her mangled corpse lay discarded in a distant corner of the basement described as a wine cellar, but really a storage area in a dark room. The right side of her head had suffered a blow severe enough to embed bone fragments into her brain as the skull fractured itself extended eight inches down the side and back of her head. The blow did not cause the little girl's death immediately. The strike from a blunt object caused internal swelling and bruising while also rendering the beautiful child as useless as a sex object. It didn't take a physician to confirm that the grotesque end of JonBenet's beauty pageant career had arrived.

The six-year-old had apparently spent the last few years of her life being exploited as an itty-bitty sexual attraction. According to physicians who read the autopsy report, injuries to JonBenet's vagina occurred weeks or months before her last assault and eventual murder. Her little hymen was a rag. Penetrations of her uterus likely occurred by intruding fingers. The vagina showed signs of abrasions from molestation long before the night of Christmas 1996. No family would wish to hear or see published the depraved details of JonBenet's sexual abuse. Without the extraordinary power of money to orchestrate a ruse and counter intuitive story of an intruder, JonBenet's sickening family secrets might well have gathered traction for the public and raised an unignorable demand for "justice."

Although any child's death would naturally attract curiosity and attention, gruesome news gatherers of the tabloid world exploited the confluence of a very wealthy family, a former Miss America contestant, and the lustful readership the tabloid press nourishes and serves. Justice is not what the tabloids pedal. Depravity handled deftly rolled the tabloid presses and made the world go around, printing money from advertising sales and spiking readership that the calculated commercial handling of JonBenet's fate produced. The traditional news outlets of the late 20th century, such as radio, television, newspapers, and magazines, operated in a more conservative era when the internet was just in its infancy. They sought to inform with editorial candor but refrained from passing judgement.

On the other hand, the tabloid formula for news reporting emphasized big red headlines, photographs with a punch, and quotations for shock and gore that outweighed

Prostitution of Justice

professional demands for social grace, or at least attention to the concept of "innocent until proven guilty." The legal complexities of prosecutions were for lawyers, most of whom did not read tabloids unless a client made the headlines. As long as the mystery sold newspapers, whether solved or exploited—JonBenet's peculiar circumstances captivated a worldwide audience. In this case, although newspapers bought ink by the barrel, John Ramsey had the money to match them. He could and did hire a legal team to sit at the table and placed his bet that he had enough gold, and therefore clout, to publish his version of the story.

The value of sex, murder, and fame cannot be underestimated in the American mind, nor does any media ignore the value of its exploitation. Within 24 hours of the first broadcast of the murder of a six-year-old beauty pageant winner, born to a former Miss West Virginia and fathered by a man with a billion dollar company, the mouths of kiddy porn enthusiasts began to water. The world of journalism exploded like a worldwide firebombing. Tabloid magazines hungering for fresh meat after the spectacular profitability of the O.J. Simpson trial virtually parachuted editors and photographers into Boulder, Colorado, for the scoops to come.

Boulder, a boisterous, hip, and sheltered college town, awoke to gangs of electronic, print, and tabloid reporters infiltrating the city. Robin Williams, in the television comedy Mork and Mindy, gave Boulder's residents a self-image of

Prostitution of Justice

being "cool." The visage of the grotesque torture of an innocent fairytale princess stung the citizens of Boulder who lived in a wealthy playground removed from the grit and crime of big cities. Even the Boulder Police Department (Boulder P.D.) was unprepared for this one-of-a-kind grisly murder of a child from one of its elite families.

JonBenet's nine-year-old brother, Burke, was awake at 5:52 a.m. on the morning of December 26, 1996, when Patsy made her 911 call. An enhanced examination of the 911 recording identified Burke's voice, saying, "What DID you find?" On such a calamitous morning during such a vital phone call, it is odd, strikingly odd, that John and Patsy claimed their son was asleep at that moment. Much later, after every detail of that morning came under scrutiny, the odd "misremembering" of Burke's presence during the call sinks in value. It becomes only one more curiosity in a scandal of curiosities while years lap up important facts, and they enter into the digestive tract of "curious" remnants of a "true crime" mythology.

"We're not talking to you," John responds. That exchange makes the couple's claim that Burke was asleep not just odd but suspicious. Why would any parent not speak to a kidnapped child's brother? The older brother's bedroom shared the second-floor suite with his sister's bedroom and playroom between them. Could he have heard the kidnapper? Should the parents ask if he heard anything before denying he was awake at the time of the call for help?

Patsy said she found the three-page ransom note neatly arrayed on the stairway leading to the kitchen. In that three-page letter, the "kidnappers" threatened to "behead" her daughter if they so much as talked to a "stray dog." Nevertheless, Patsy talked and talked a lot. She not only called 911 but also had close friends:[1] Fleet and Priscilla White, John and Barbara Fernie, their minister, Rol Hoverstock, JonBenet's pediatrician, Dr. Francesco Beuf, and his wife, Penni. She asked them all to come to the home. She also contacted her sister, Pam Paugh, and parents, Don, and Nedra Paugh in Atlanta. Nedra was the beauty contestant's family matriarch. Pam Paugh also competed in pageants and won Miss West Virginia in 1980 after Patsy's crowning in 1977.

Before the guests could arrive, the Ramseys provided Officer Rick French, the first Boulder police officer on the scene, with the ransom note. "Note" hardly describes the 376 words of this bizarre ransom demand. Unlike a typical brief and curt ransom note, the writer's personality flowed through the ink, full of confidence and imagination. Despite the claim of coming from a "small foreign faction," it was anything but foreign in its phraseology. The letter grows immensely threatening and personal.

Mr. Ramsey,

Prostitution of Justice

Listen carefully! We are a group of individuals that represent a small foreign faction. We [word crossed out] respect your business but not the country that it serves. At this time, we have your daughter in our possession. She is safe and unharmed and if you want her to see 1997, you must follow our instructions to the letter. You will withdraw $118,000.00 from your account. $100,000 will be in $100 bills, and the remaining $18,000 in $20 bills. Make sure that you bring an adequate size attaché to the bank. When you get home, you will put the money in a brown paper bag. I will call you between 8 and 10 am tomorrow to instruct you on delivery. The delivery will be exhausting, so I advise you to be rested. If we monitor you getting the money early, we might call you early to arrange an earlier delivery of the money and, hence, an earlier [word crossed out] pick up of your daughter. ["delivery" scratched out] Any deviation from my instructions will result in the immediate execution of your daughter. You will also be deprived of her remains or proper burial. The two gentlemen watching over your daughter do not particularly like you, so I advise you not to provoke them. Speaking to anyone about your situation, such as police, F.B.I., etc., will result in your daughter being beheaded. If we catch you talking to a stray dog, she dies. If you alert bank authorities, she dies. If the money is in any way marked or tampered with, she dies. You will be searched for electronic devices, and if any are found, she dies. You can try to deceive us but be warned that we are familiar with law enforcement countermeasures and tactics. You stand

Prostitution of Justice

a 99% chance of killing your daughter if you try to outsmart us. Follow our instructions, and you stand a 100% chance of getting her back. You and your family are under constant scrutiny, as are the authorities. Don't try to grow a brain, John. You are not the only fat cat around, so don't think that killing will be difficult. Don't underestimate us, John. Use that good Southern common sense of yours. It is up to you now, John!

Victory! S.B.T.C.

Prostitution of Justice

Chapter Two: Contamination

By the time Patsy Ramsey made her 911 call for help, as the autopsy report has since revealed, JonBenet already lay cold and dead. Six-year-old JonBenet Ramsey had been bludgeoned, garroted, and sexually assaulted in her own home, and her mangled corpse was left to cool in the distant wine cellar. The killer violated her vagina postmortem with one of Patsy's paintbrushes, leaving the mutilated body with a red heart drawn on the palm of her hand. Patsy had often drawn those red hearts on JonBenet's palm most nights at bedtime. The dead child wore a blouse decorated with sequins and a silver star with a ligature, strung tight as barbed wire a half inch deep into the child's neck.

Dr. John Meyer, Boulder County Coroner, described an eight-and-a-half inch-long fracture from the top of JonBenet's head moving downward and back behind her right ear, a blow sufficient to have felled a 300-pound man. The "control device," the garrote, was embedded a half inch into the little girl's neck and came from Patsy's art supplies, located near the entry to the obscure storage room. That room was also used as a wine cellar, next to the crawl space, dark and buried away in the southwest corner of the mansion, a hidden crime scene, later disturbed by John Ramsey.

Prostitution of Justice

The ransom note Patsy "found" threatened to "behead" her daughter if the parents so much as spoke to a "stray dog." Yet, Patsy not only called 911, but she talked with friends, inviting them over to their home despite the clear language of the "kidnappers:" "You and your family are under constant scrutiny as well as the authorities." The guests who would contaminate the crime scene included Fleet and Priscilla White, John and Barbara Fernie, their minister, Rol Hoverstock, JonBenet's pediatrician, Dr. Francesco Beuf, and his wife, Penni. She also contacted her sister, Pam Paugh, and parents, Don and Nedra Paugh. Nedra was the beauty contestant's family matriarch.

The Ramseys provided Officer Rick French, the first Boulder police officer on the scene, with the ransom note. "Note" hardly describes the 376 words of this bizarre ransom demand. Unlike a typical ransom note, the writer's personality flowed through the ink, full of confidence and imagination. Furthermore, it was anything but foreign in its phrasing. The letter was immensely threatening and personal.

The police should have taken the threats of the kidnappers more seriously, as well as the parents. The hysterical phone call didn't cause the police to think to park squad cars anyplace other than around the house while alerting everyone in the neighborhood that something had occurred, including any kidnappers.

Prostitution of Justice

It seems peculiar that the Ramseys did not wait for help from law enforcement to arrive. The first cop arrived in 4 minutes, but soon after, Patsy's other guests arrived to fill the house with their DNA, fingerprints, and hair samples. The outward behavior of the parents appeared inconsistent with a belief that their daughter had been kidnapped. Of course, Patsy was hysterical and in uncontrollable despair when they first greeted Officer French. Guests showed the officer where Patsy claimed she found the note on the stairway leading to the second floor. In such a dramatic scene, Patsy needed the comfort of her friends with whom they had celebrated Christmas the night before. Yet, under her puffy eyes and Kleenex, the stylish hostess hid her face while still wearing the same red sweater she had worn to the Christmas party 12 hours earlier at the Whites' home.

John, always described as courteous, displayed the confidence of a CEO—no tears nor rage, just working on the problem. With his banking relationship, he arranged for the cash the morning after Christmas from his broker at Merrill Lynch as if it were a regular Monday morning in New York City instead of the Christmas holiday in a mountain town. Some contradictions in his behavior and the demands of the ransom note may have occurred to the brilliant former Navy officer and uber tech wizard. But the invited crowd, despite the warnings in the ransom note, stands out as peculiar, at least. Any professional police department, as well as any truly desperate parents of a kidnapped child, should have paused, considering the threats of beheading JonBenet. The presence of so many cops and friends could have tipped off the kidnappers, who claimed to be monitoring events as the street and driveway filled with traffic.

Anyone with a television or a radio would have been at least remotely aware of the spectacle of the O.J. Simpson trial, which had only concluded on October 3, 1995, months before JonBenet's death. In relation to criminal investigations in the United States, a person would undoubtedly have learned of the Los Angeles Police Department's crime laboratory and its reputation as a "cesspool of contamination." It helped Simpson's lawyers win an acquittal. Fortunately for the kidnapper, when Officer Rick French arrived on the scene at 5:56 a.m. and parked in front of the home, he failed to find JonBenet's body in his search. Although he was looking for evidence of kidnapping and assumed the girl was missing, his cursory search of the mansion failed to fully explore the basement where she lay dead.

Misdirection and incompetence played the starring roles in the made-for-TV opening moments of the investigation. Throughout the unfolding chaos, JonBenet's corpse lay undisturbed down the stairs in the basement, through the boiler room, into a dark corner of a storage room and makeshift wine cellar. There, she awaited discovery, out of cursory view as she lay behind to the left of the opened door. Officer French, of

Prostitution of Justice

course, was searching for a little girl or evidence of a "kidnapping," not a corpse. The Ramseys' guests had also begun arriving for the sudden and terrible social event with first responders, making an Agatha Christie-like mystery gathering at a mansion high on "The Hill," a tony neighborhood overlooking the CU Boulder campus and eastern horizon.

What typically happens in every other case involving a missing child? The police treat the entire house, grounds, and persons as a crime scene. They take names, separate the parents, and obtain their statements. They may take them downtown for further information and investigation while detectives and the forensics team search for evidence. Child welfare officials privately interview any siblings from the home in a controlled, recorded, private environment. Anyone who walks into the scene not relevant to the ongoing case is listed on a log sheet, and even if family, friends, or clergy should arrive, they are invited to leave. If a dead child is discovered, everyone becomes a witness or a suspect.

Given the statistics on missing children later found victims of child abuse or dead, the parents should by then have been treated courteously, but as potential suspects. Boulder cops and brass first on the scene remarkably failed to seriously question the oddity of so long a note: its stylistic peculiarities, the "kidnapper's" use of a pen belonging to the Ramseys on a pad of paper belonging to the Ramseys, and a practice note! The victimized family permitted copies of the note to be made and distributed among the guests. John kept his military-trained head cool under that morning's stress. It seemed that Patsy, a woman of leisure, art, and drama, could not be consoled. Could she have presented an inconsolable state? Patsy had performed a dramatic interpretation during the talent component for her Miss America performance.

More questions surfaced that day and remain unanswered a quarter of a century later. What kidnapper plans a break-in and kidnapping but fails to bring a ransom note? In a crime scene where time is presumably of the essence, what was the need for a practice note? Why write the longest ransom note in history? Why not grab the kid, dead or alive, to secure the ransom? Each elapsing second increased the kidnapper's likelihood of detection, but the kidnappers seemed oddly unconcerned that the parents may wake and spoil the crime.

The FBI agents who arrived later that morning had noticed peculiarities in the ransom note, beginning with its length and the odd, personal concern for John to be well-rested before delivering the ransom. As if a relative or close friend of John's—or perhaps with sarcasm—the writer advised, "Use that good Southern common sense of yours."

John Ramsey was a midwestern Yankee who grew up in Lincoln, Nebraska, where he was born on December 7, 1943. After high school, he migrated to Michigan to obtain a degree in electrical engineering from Michigan State University. He served his country in the United States Navy as an officer,

Prostitution of Justice

including three years at Subic Bay in the Philippine Islands. He went on to take an MBA at the University of Michigan in 1971, later moving to Atlanta in the South. His "good Southern common sense" was a popular jest in the household from his Southern-born and bred wife, Patsy, and her family.

In short order, more police arrived for the kidnapping investigation. The Boulder Police Department was unusually thin in the upscale college town during the Christmas break. The lead officer on the scene was Commander John Eller. It was his call to inform the Denver Police Department that his understaffed college town police department could handle the investigation. He did not need nor accept assistance from the nearby metropolis 35 miles south that routinely handled murder investigations. JonBenet's death was the first murder in Boulder that year.

Along with the ransom note, the search had turned up a partially filled bowl of pineapple. That bowl would later reveal Burke's and Patsy's fingerprints, not JonBenet's, even though pineapple was her favorite fruit and was found in her stomach during the autopsy. Cops found no pry marks on the doors—an examination John Ramsey requested—thus revealing no forced entry.

Since kidnapping is a federal crime, the FBI was called. John obtained the ransom money through his contacts with Merrill Lynch, and all waited for the kidnapper's call amid Patsy's fervent prayers and tears. FBI agents watched the home filled with guests, joining police officers throughout the mansion, all contaminating the crime scene. The Federal agents had the wherewithal to continue their investigation, and the agency discovered that the writer had used a pen and pad of paper at home for the note, then neatly replaced the pen in its desk container.[2] Meanwhile, they observed the bereaved couple. John was remarkably composed, opening his mail at his desk. Patsy covered her face with Kleenex, sobbed, and shook her head. She was seemingly distraught, quite dramatic, and surrounded by girlfriends.

Prostitution of Justice

Chapter Three: Credible Millionaires

Commander John Eller was a medium-sized man with military-cut short blond hair, a 28-year police professional. He came to Boulder from Florida as a lieutenant in 1979, replacing the hot weather in Florida with the seasonal college town of Boulder, Colorado. In his 18 years at Boulder P.D., he had risen to Commander and had begun working as a detective only 11 months earlier. As a rookie detective with a Police Commander's rank, he decided not to separate the parents and question them individually, advising Boulder P.D. officers at the scene that the couple with the missing six-year-old daughter were "Credible Millionaires" and thus free of suspicion. The absent child and bizarre note indicated nothing of parental involvement in Commander John Eller's mind. The initial investigation had turned up nothing of interest to the career police officer who couldn't wait for a forensic examination. He could think of little to do until the kidnapper made contact.

Eller and other officers on the scene, oblivious to evidence contamination, permitted friends and family to wander about the crime scene, comforting the victimized parents and waiting for that call promised by the kidnapper to come between 8:00 a.m. and 10:00 a.m. Perhaps the gleam of the $118,000 ransom demand in the note dulled as the kidnapper may have noticed that Boulder P.D. had surrounded the house and the Ramseys filled it with friends of the Ramseys.

The writer of the note revealed an odd heritage and criminal modesty and claimed to be only a "small foreign faction." Some of the braggadocio did appear in the pages filled with gruesome analyses of politics, death, and grief. As the FBI pointed out, kidnappers, least of all those from a "small foreign faction," do not waste time on their target's emotional issues or their well-being, at least so far as the FBI's experience and records had been kept.

"The delivery will be exhausting, so I advise you to be rested." A note may warn of electronic screening, but most kidnappers don't give a damn about the bagman's rest. Notes do demand a ransom, but $118,000 is an odd number to place on any parents' irreplaceable child, especially for a victim whose company, the *Boulder Daily Camera,* recently reported had grossed a billion dollars. Coincidentally or fortuitously, $118,000 was John Ramsey's bonus that year. His family wouldn't be too damaged financially. That is one very considerate "small foreign faction."

This particular day after Christmas, Eller was short-staffed. Many detectives, forensic specialists, and patrol officers had taken Christmas holiday leave. Most of the University of Colorado's out-of-state and in-state students had traveled home for the holidays. Still, Boulder is more than the host city for the CU Buffaloes. The small city had begun to

Prostitution of Justice

awaken, some homes celebrating with toys, sweets, and new clothes, others nursing hangovers, some with unresolved family spats calling 911 to report a barking dog, a homeless schizophrenic, a fender bender, or a reckless driver—normal day-to-day crimes. This mystery of kidnapping and international terrorism evoked something bigger than the city had ever experienced. John and Patsy Ramsey touched the rookie investigator's heart, and John Eller's "credible millionaires" needed to grieve.

Eller called for a break in the investigation until Boulder's detectives and forensic units could respond and the DA's office alerted. He left Detective Linda Arndt, a specialist in Victim Assistance, to monitor the premises in the interim and provide guidance when responding to the kidnapper's phone call. With a remarkable display of inexperience, Eller permitted all the guests to remain and continue their contamination of the crime scene.

Detective Arndt, a blonde, raw-boned woman, saw less of grieving parents than had the Commander. She saw that Patsy and John did not hold each other nor even spend time in the same rooms. Priscilla White and Barbara Fernie attended to Patsy, trying to console the inconsolable. John paced the living room and the den, with husbands banding together with the aloof and mannerly businessman.

Fleet White, John's closest friend with whom he enjoyed yachting, of his own accord searched the basement. He found nothing, even though he had proceeded as far back as the darkened storage room. During White's venture into the basement, he noticed a hole in the basement window but thought little of it. Like Boulder P.D. Officer Rick French, White never entered the darkened storage room where JonBenet's remains lay hidden.

Sometime before noon, long after the 10:00 a.m. deadline, John "disappeared" for a short time, according to Detective Arndt. Perhaps he searched for his daughter. Perhaps shattered but strong, he needed to compose himself. John, the former Naval officer, exuded strength. His eyes could promote a person or dismiss a crowd with a glance. At this point, Boulder P.D. had done nothing to return his daughter or convince him they would. The officers at the mansion had not turned up a single item of evidence pointing to an intruder in their several hours on site. In fact, the home's interior and exterior indicated no evidence of an intruder's break-in, down to the cobwebs on the basement window or footprints in the fresh and quickly melting snow.

Detective Commander John Eller had never investigated a homicide, nor had he handled many kidnappings or terrorist plots. He'd seen plenty of domestic violence and drunken campus pranksters, but no investigator anywhere had seen a ransom note as weird as this "small foreign faction." Nevertheless, Eller made terrible decisions for a street cop,

Prostitution of Justice

confused directions for a detective, and performed miserably as a police commander.

First, he never separated and questioned the parents, a basic decision even a rookie would have known to make. Second, he never treated the premises as a crime scene, nor did he seal it off. Third, Eller and all the other officers should never have permitted friends and family to tramp around the house, contaminate the scene, park their cars in the driveway, and alert anyone and everyone in the neighborhood that something big and serious had happened at Ramsey's home. Overconfident in his officers and his command, Eller rejected the help offered by the Denver Police Department Detectives, who called Boulder P.D. as soon as D.P.D. learned of it. When the FBI discovered a practice note in the kitchen along with the pad and pen used, Eller failed to connect the possibility that someone familiar with the home and the kitchen may have had a hand in the mysterious note and kidnapping.

During the next several hours after Eller shut down the investigation and sent his police officers and the FBI packing, the lone detective, Linda Arndt, haplessly carried out her assignment. Trained to comfort and protect victims of crimes, she moved about, keeping her eyes open but feeling hopelessly outnumbered. She made numerous calls for backup and received none as the grieving parents and friends roamed the house freely. The child abduction played out for three excruciating hours; the crowd moved about, wittingly and unwittingly spreading their hair and fibers. Officer Rick French hadn't found long-dead JonBenet; thus, a medical examiner hadn't been called, nor a crime scene declared, closed off, and protected. Eller treated the matter as a kidnapping and ransom that victimized the tragic small market of the very rich.

Detective Linda Arndt, an 11-year veteran of the Boulder Police Department, could not single-handedly monitor such a crowd as tension grew in the rooms. Patsy Ramsey cried endlessly, her face in her hands; she occasionally opened her fingers to peek at the response of the crowd. The ransom note passed from hand to hand; photocopies were made and distributed among the guests.

Arndt reports John as courteous, always courteous, though he appeared nervous to the detective after his brief disappearance once the authorities left. In fact, John did not disappear. Arndt simply lost track of him. The detective could not monitor everyone present, and John's absence could have been nothing more than a traumatized man unable to sit still. Nevertheless, Arndt had noticed a change in John's cool, commanding visage. He sat at his desk reviewing mail, his toes bouncing his heel in an unconscious nervous shaking.

At 1:00 p.m., Arndt suggested John search the house again. Confident and rangy like John Wayne, Fleet White accompanied him on the search. Arndt warned them not to disturb anything if they made any discovery, and a remarkably short search began. John Ramsey went immediately to the

Prostitution of Justice

basement stairway and descended to head straight through the boiler room hallway with Fleet White steps behind him. They proceeded to the storage room/wine cellar. The boiler room door opens forward, obscuring light into the adjacent corner storage room.

"Oh, my God," John cried into the dark room and rushed to JonBenet's stiffened, ravaged, but clothed corpse. He ripped the black tape from her blue lips. Fleet White had entered the room and touched the girl's cold foot. Horror struck. He retreated from the basement and its ghastly secret, then up the stairs, yelling, "Call 911." John had picked up his daughter's body by the waist, still wrapped in a blanket, arms upraised in rigor mortis, and rushed the corpse away from the hidden cellar room, back through the hallway and up the stairs, all while holding his daughter's stiff body at arm's length like a department store mannequin.

Arndt ordered Ramsey to put the body down near the front door and told White to guard the stairwell. Guests began to rush forward, gasping, and terror struck. Patsy remained in the living room initially, hysterical and in shambles or dissembling. Kidnapping had become murder.

Linda Arndt checked the body for signs of life and found none and no smell of decay.[3] The unassisted victim assistance officer, in the choke and horror of the moment, removed JonBenet's body to under the Christmas tree. Untrained in homicide investigations, she had twice removed

Prostitution of Justice

the body to create a third compromised and contaminated crime scene. Worse, Arndt covered the horrid sight with a blanket, perhaps soothing the stunned faces and gulping eyes but further contaminating evidence. She made damaging errors, the kind of errors as those of criminologists in the Los Angeles Police Department, that "cesspool of contamination," that had led to the recent acquittal of O.J. Simpson. Arndt was not a criminologist and would initially suffer the blame for the bungled investigation by the department's higher-ups. She resigned from Boulder P.D. as the department designated her as a scapegoat and soon sued Boulder's finest for their conduct in assassinating her character.

Back at the Ramsey mansion, the household and guests cringed in horror, sickened at John and Fleet's discovery. Patsy Ramsey, now completely traumatized, cried out to God to raise her daughter from the dead as He had Lazarus. Reverend Rol Hoverstock led the assembled group in the Lord's Prayer. Linda Arndt joined, knowing she was completely unable to manage the crowd. Soon after the prayer, Fleet White departed, returning to the basement where he and John Ramsey had discovered the murder. He picked up the black tape that had covered JonBenet's mouth, examined it briefly, and then dropped the evidence, inadvertently adding more contamination to the newly revealed crime scene.

Arndt recalled vividly years later, during a nationally televised interview, when she and John Ramsey knelt over

Prostitution of Justice

JonBenet's body, John stared with stone-cold blue eyes, inscrutable, and with a look so frightening that the police officer mentally counted the number of bullets in her service weapon[4]. She only had a cell phone, not a police radio, and her calls slowly connected her to report the murder. Boulder P.D. Officer Berry Weiss arrived at 1:20 p.m., and the mansion was soon filled again with police and emptied of guests.

Now that JonBenet Ramsey had reappeared in the mansion murdered, the ransom note and the intentions of a "small foreign faction" began to come under inquiry. John Ramsey's menacing eyes had raised Detective Linda Arndt's antennae, and by then, John had contacted his Boulder friend and business lawyer, Mike Bynum. The attorney properly advised Ramsey to remain silent and helped John and Patsy to employ the phenomenal criminal defense firm of Haddon, Morgan, and Foreman.

The discovery of JonBenet's body stashed in the basement did not cause Commander John Eller, rookie Detective of the Boulder P. D., to direct his officers to continue to treat the Ramseys as anything other than victims, a truly perplexing decision: No call from the kidnappers, a corpse underneath the Christmas tree, and a fantastical ransom note that seemed now to be a diversion or to represent a spectacular blunder.

No matter the curiosities, the devastated couple, now represented by counsel, were permitted to leave the house and

Prostitution of Justice

received the treatment of "credible millionaires," as Eller had described them. From that moment forward, the second-guessing started and has never ended.

Prostitution of Justice

Chapter Four: Quandaries

Who wrote that ransom note? What did JonBenet do to deserve having a human being smash her head in, strangle her, and abandon her body in a depiction of necrophilia and obscene gratification by torturing the child beauty princess in her own home? Where did JonBenet die? Did her last breath occur in the cellar, the kitchen, her bedroom, the playroom? When did the kidnapping turn to torture and murder, an abandonment of the original plan? Why leave the 45-pound corpse and forgo a $118,000 payday after crafting so detailed a ransom note? Was a kidnapping only staged to hide a poorly concealed corpse, and was the body mutilated to reveal inconceivable acts of savagery? What was the motive for the six-year-old child's debasement and infliction of barbaric carnage on the victim? Why weren't John and Patsy Ramsey separated and questioned when Boulder P.D. first arrived? How did the criminal justice system in Boulder, Colorado, become so twisted that the prime suspects would be offered a private cabin within the criminal justice system?

Patsy cried over the telephone, screaming for help during the 911 call. The parents reported that Burke had been and remained asleep when Officer Rick French arrived. Officer French found Burke sleeping or pretending to sleep when he checked the boy's bedroom. Burke's bedroom shared the

Prostitution of Justice

playroom between his sister's bedroom and his. The stealthy kidnapper, moving with the powers of a Jedi Knight, had removed his sister from her nearby bedroom and left a ransom note. John and Patsy claim Burke slept through it all. Wouldn't either of the frantic parents wake their sleeping child to ask, "Do you know where JonBenet is? Is she in your room? Did you hear anything, Burke?"

It was odd, and struck investigators as odd, that the parents did not wake their son after finding the ransom note. Then, months later, authorities sought and obtained an enhanced audio of the 911 call to learn that Burke was awake and present during the crisis at the moment of the call. He is heard asking, "What do you want me to do?" John, known for a cool demeanor and even cooler head, demonstrated his self-control in his reaction: "We're not talking to you."

The ransom demand of $118,000 amounted to little more or less than the value of John's sailboat, the Miss America. John also had one of his private jet airplanes at his disposal for his family's flight to Michigan on the morning of December 26, 1996. Quite oddly, but not oddly enough, police didn't see John's eagerness to leave the state as a "probable cause" to initiate questioning. John had called his pilot that morning to proceed with his plans to fly to Michigan with his family that tragic morning. Boulder Police, in a moment of professional competence, realized that the man's desire to leave the state in the critical hours of his daughter's kidnapping did not present a

Prostitution of Justice

typical concern and response to the circumstances. Since a crime had occurred and flight from the scene of a crime is often an indicator of a guilty conscience, police authorities informed John that he wouldn't be leaving Colorado's jurisdiction and flying away to Charlevoix, Michigan.

Forensic examination revealed that the black tape removed from JonBenet's mouth showed no evidence that JonBenet was alive when it was placed over her lips. What was the reason for the tape? Staging? So it appeared. But that black piece of tape had more to tell. Curiously, clothing fibers from someone present at the time the tape was applied lay stuck on the adhesive side. How curious that those fibers matched the clothing Patsy wore to the White's Christmas party. Compounding that curiosity, Patsy still wore the red sweater she had worn at the White's Christmas party the following morning of the kidnapping when she greeted Officer French. Had some "intruder" worn or brought Patsy's clothing into the proximity of the deceased child and the black tape immediately before placing it over the child's mouth postmortem, then returned the clothing to the parents' bedroom for Patsy to wear it again the following morning? Reasonable people could wonder if Patsy had slept in her clothing or failed to sleep at all the evening before, too "busy" preparing the guise of kidnapping throughout the night and into the morning to change before she "discovered" the ransom note on the stairway.

Prostitution of Justice

A crime such as murder involving torture, sexual assault, and strangulation requires time, as does writing a three-page ransom note, and practice as well. Considering the time between 10 p.m. when the family arrived home and the discovery of the ransom note a little before 6:00 a.m., how much evidence appeared, disappeared, was compromised, or cleansed? The sheets from JonBenet's bed were not those the housekeeper, Linda Pugh, had put on Christmas morning. Did the kidnapper change the linen? Could other areas of the home have been cleaned? And there was a cleanup. Forty days after the investigation began, on February 5, 1997, as reported in the *Denver Post*[5], the killer appeared to have wiped the body but did not entirely wash the corpse.

Adding to the argument that this kidnapping was staged, one asks if the perpetrator reasonably thought that the body might not be discovered until it began to decompose. Leaving a ransom note assured massive local, state, and federal police scrutiny. Why use a bizarre strangulation to finish off JonBenet so savagely? One explanation for the construction of the control device and the knots used to strangle the child arose as the instructions for knotting the strangulation apparatus are found in the Boy Scout's Manual. Burke was in the Boy Scouts. John Ramsey had also been teaching Burke to tie knots as he "showed him the ropes" for sailing the family yacht, the Miss America. The brutal application of the rope as a garrote opens up speculations as to the studies of the offender. After entering

Prostitution of Justice

the house and having committed a murder-torture of a little girl, couldn't the kidnapper(s) have left the grounds with an extra forty-five pounds to retain the possibility of a $118,000 ransom?

Did the parents fail to realize, ignore, or anticipate that crowding their house may bring into doubt evidence pointing to a criminal intruder, one who would soon be sought as a murderer? The immediate violation of all the terms of the ransom note creates the inference that the Ramseys knew JonBenet was not in possession of some "small foreign faction." The couple's separation from each other through the morning did not comport with spouses who typically cling to each other in their hope for the return of their child.

Did an earlier disappearance by John, noted by Detective Linda Arndt, from the gathering of friends have anything to do with a staged kidnapping, JonBenet's corpse, or a disturbance of some incriminating evidence? Could a bright person have shrewdly, rather than carelessly, cleaned up, set up, or tainted the crime scene?

The Ramseys identified employees of both John's business and Patsy's housekeeper as suspects. Did someone "inside" John Ramsey's company attempt to snatch away his bonus at the price of his daughter's life? What parents, with this couple's wealth, would not have paid a million dollars or two million dollars to see their child alive? $118,000 placed an odd value on JonBenet's life. Why not $100,000, or $200,000, or $1,000,000?

Dr. John Meyer performed the autopsy on JonBenet on the morning of December 27, 1996. In addition to the causes of death—strangulation and blunt trauma to the head—he found acute and chronic vaginal trauma. The autopsy report provides a gruesome picture of JonBenet's last months as well as her last minutes. John and Patsy, through their phalanx of lawyers, public relations firm, and published spin, fought against the release of this report as they had fought against the release of any evidence since the beginning of the investigation. How could they explain or deny chronic vaginal trauma in a six-year-old?

A single episode of rape or sexual assault on the night of her murder could not explain the evidence of chronic abuse, nor does a child's vaginitis prove chronic abuse. The Ramseys' pediatrician and close friend, Dr. Francesco Beuf, did not view vaginitis as evidence of chronic sexual abuse. How did he explain it, or did he deny it? Did he ever say from a medical point of view how or why her hymen was reduced to a rag and the wall of her vagina repeatedly abraded? No, Dr. Beuf never said publicly more than that the child appeared to be "much loved."

The Ramseys explained that JonBenet's thirty-three visits to her pediatrician in the last three years of her life were because of her mild asthma and the fact that they had very good health insurance, which they did not hesitate to use. Dr. Beuf reported "mild" vaginitis. Could this have been caused by her bedwetting problem? Surely, Dr. Beuf knew of it. Did Dr. Beuf also know that JonBenet would leave feces in her bed? Vaginitis does not prove chronic sexual abuse. Yet, chronic sexual abuse could explain vaginitis in a child of JonBenet's age. Soiling the bed with feces is known to occur when a child victim tries to make herself unattractive. Additionally, chronic vaginitis means the vaginitis had been continuous and ongoing, repeated with such frequency that the child's vagina did not have time to heal.

Vaginitis, however, present in a little girl, does not present the same symptoms as chronic sexual abuse, although it may arise from molestation. The autopsy did not identify JonBenet's "mild vaginitis" as a possible source for the signs of chronic abrasive penetration because it was not a possible source. Only someone with frequent intimate access to JonBenet could explain the condition documented by Dr. Meyer's autopsy. Additionally, the six-year-old's vagina was measured at one-by-one centimeters, about twice the size of the opening of the average six-year-old girl.

Long after JonBenet should have been potty trained, certainly as late as the fall of 1994, her toileting behavior was odd. By 1995, in addition to more frequent soiling of her bed with feces and urine, JonBenet often did not want to use toilet tissue on herself. On occasion she would call out to adults, "wipe, wipe," for assistance. This might help to explain the vaginitis but not the curiously immature behavior in a bright and extraordinarily precocious child.

Dr. Beuf spoke out on behalf of his wealthy personal friends, the Ramseys, to deny sexual abuse. He clearly had a vested interest in doing so because if he had suspected or identified child sexual abuse and had failed to report that suspicion, the autopsy findings would have exposed his complicity or stupidity, since his patient had turned up sexually tortured and dead. The Ramseys' selective use of the testimony and/or friendly opinions of personal attendants such as Dr. and Mrs. Beuf, family friend Susan Stine, and John's older children and his former wife does not explain away clear scientific evidence of chronic trauma to JonBenet's vagina. Was JonBenet used for sexual gratification long before her murder? Was this not relevant to the murder investigation?

When parents, even rich parents, report a kidnapping that turns into murder with an extraordinary ransom note, antennae go up, and the surrounding circumstances become part of the probable cause for arrest. When John Ramsey immediately went to JonBenet's body, disturbed everything he was told not to disturb, and frightened the daylights out of the police officer on duty, some pauses should have occurred in the "victim" treatment the Ramseys had received.

Commander John Eller of the Boulder Police Department incomprehensibly directed his officers to continue

Prostitution of Justice

to treat the Ramseys as victims, a truly perplexing decision given JonBenet's corpse underneath the Christmas tree. There clearly had been no kidnapping, yet Eller, with his application of victimhood to the "credible millionaires," calls into question the equal application of the law according to the social status of the suspects. Eller ignored culpability with parents who had money. Would he then assume that poor parents must likely be more culpable and assumed guilty?

Prostitution of Justice

Chapter Five: The Gold Rush

Overnight, reporters, editors, photographers, producers, and freelancers from around the world discovered the picturesque City of Boulder, home of the University of Colorado; young, scenic, and JonBenet Ramsey's death the first and only, but the most spectacular Boulder homicide in all of 1996. Six days later, the Ramseys granted an interview to CNN's Brien Cabell on January 1, 1997. That scoop, with an apparently unscripted appearance on nationwide television, shook the story out of Boulder, shocked viewers, and quite likely Ramsey's lawyers, while making the world salivate for answers to the JonBenet Ramsey murder mystery.

John praised the Boulder Police and said they had been "wonderful,"[6] although the couple had yet to give statements to Boulder Detectives (on the advice of counsel). They did present themselves as united in their innocence and professed their desire to find the perpetrator of JonBenet's murder. Patsy still could not stop crying and raised doubts the interview had meant to quell. Patsy's tearful, subliminal mention of Susan Smith, a Texas woman who had drowned her two young sons, raised eyebrows nationally. Some asked if Patsy was on medications. Is John too strong? Why talk to CNN and not Boulder P.D.?

Lawyers, especially top-drawer criminal defense lawyers, prefer the camera on them if there must be a camera and not an unscripted interview that creates "facts" and "images" outside their control and the potential jury pool. The law firm of Haddon, Morgan, and Foreman had to initiate damage control. They immediately sent the Ramseys to a top-drawer Washington D.C. public relations firm, the now-defunct Rowan & Blewitt, from which John and Patsy hired Pat Korton, a crisis management expert.

The public relations spin began with an argument that no one knows how a parent would react under the same circumstances as the Ramseys. Korton then used the family's affiliation with St. John's Episcopal Church, the Rev. Rol Hoverstock as a friend, and the congregation as a symbol of moral values as opposed to the immoral character of journalists, like a flock of vultures circling Boulder. Prior to religious services at St. John's for JonBenet on January 5, 1997, Pat Korton called the media to invite them for a Ramsey photo opportunity. Reverend Hoverstock, the close family friend, again told his congregation that he saw the parents' suffering and believed in their innocence.

After the service, Korton directed the congregation through the front doors. It appeared to the legion of cameras and reporters as though the congregation acted as human shields, protecting their own families and the Ramseys, united against the unsympathetic, suspicious mudslingers. John and Patsy appeared to walk a gauntlet between rows of aggressive cameramen and reporters, with the congregants acting as human shields to the floodlights and microphones of the press that Korton had invited. Working with the public relations team, the Haddon, Morgan, and Foreman law firm labeled all media that covered the staged event as "tabloids."

With orchestrated hypocrisy, any public relations gaffes arising from the CNN interview had been blunted, and a human shield of worshipful camera fodder from the back rows to the pulpit protected the bereaved couple and Burke as they departed the church. Pat Korton, a true master of his profession, replaced and reshaped the images from calls for a lynching to a completely refocused subject of outrage – the press. As opposed to the carpetbaggers of the press, the Ramseys presented their decency and humility as the decency of Boulder. With the show of the congregation's support, all of Boulder appeared as the "Decent People," and all the press, print, electronic, and especially tabloids represented maggots.

According to that manufactured and mass-reproduced image of values and virtues in the parents, the very depravity of torture and molestation weighed against John or Patsy, crushing the back of their beautiful girl's skull into a seven-by-four-inch depression. Nevertheless, somebody did it. The parents stated that JonBenet was asleep upon returning from the party at White's home, and they took her directly to bed. Dr. John Meyer performed JonBenet's autopsy on the morning of December 27, 1996. In addition to the causes of death, strangulation, and blunt trauma to the head, he found pineapple in her stomach and that

Prostitution of Justice

nagging acute and chronic vaginal trauma. The autopsy report provides a gruesome picture of JonBenet's last months, as well as her last minutes. John and Patsy, through their phalanx of lawyers, public relations firm, and spin, fought against the release of the autopsy report as they had fought against the release of any evidence from the beginning of the investigation, especially the ransom note.

The autopsy report indicated the presence of pineapple in JonBenet's digestive tract, and the police found a half-empty bowl of pineapple in the kitchen with Patsy's and Burke's fingerprints on it. No one served JonBenet pineapple at the party she had attended earlier that evening at the home of Fleet and Priscilla White. The parents claimed they immediately brought a sleepy JonBenet home and put her to bed. How did the pineapple get into the child's stomach shortly before her tortured death? No one has explained those pineapple remnants in JonBenet's stomach or why Patsy's and Burke's fingerprints appear on the bowl.

Despite the irrevocably compromised and contaminated crime scene, the paintbrush in the coroner's examination also revealed the fibers from the sweater Patsy wore the night before the murder. That Patsy Ramsey, with a queen's wardrobe, wore the same outfit as at the Christmas party overnight and again the morning of December 26, 1996, troubled those who knew the former Miss West Virginia. The facts coming to light that morning did not fail to raise suspicions, the menacing gaze of

Prostitution of Justice

John Ramsey did not fail to raise fear in Detective Linda Arndt, and the demonic slaughter with sexual cretinism glazed the public appetite for more and more horrifying news.

Access Graphics' full-throttled success put John and Patsy Ramsey into the height of financial security, the limelight of Boulder society, and a bull's eye for financial exploitation by the press. A life-and-death crisis had disrupted the Ramseys' lives several years before JonBenet's murder. Patsy contracted cervical cancer, and it ravaged her. Her health insurance and wealth gave her access to ovarian cancer treatments from Johns Hopkins University Hospital.

Patsy lived the life of a cancer victim and invalid. Nedra Paugh, a compact human dynamo with hands knotted from arthritis, traveled from Atlanta to Boulder. She stayed and directed Patsy's medical needs, assumed the household responsibilities and administration, and cared for the children and Patsy's bedside, to give John the time needed for his young, thriving company, which he had moved to Boulder from Atlanta.

It was John's job to make the money. He had the business and its responsibilities. Patsy's occupation was to heal, live, see her children grow up, and polish this fabulous jewel of life. While the former Miss West Virginia remained secluded at home in Boulder, Nedra protected her from visitors whose minor sniffles could invade Patsy's weakened immune system. When Patsy would see visitors, she often wore a turban at home, wigs, and scarves for travel to Baltimore to endure treatments, face the almighty blood work, and return exhausted but alive, fighting, still living with her family in Boulder. Often, family and friends, key to Patsy's happiness, brought them cooked meals. Some wondered at John's stoic visage, commanding his distance, loyal to Patsy through the ordeal. She survived. That miracle had steeled Patsy and offered the press a hook for compositions on her life's life-and-death struggles.

Each year in Boulder, Patsy replaced her white Jaguar with the current model, it seemed, but during cancer, JonBenet rode in the front seat with her father while her mother survived treatment and convalesced. While employed at Hayes Microcomputer Systems in Atlanta before children, Patsy had introduced herself as "the former Miss West Virginia." Now, the spotlight had dimmed; Patsy endured as a middle-aged cancer patient, weak, depleted, bald from radiation treatments, a former beauty, now worn and riddled with disease. The now-depleted Miss West Virginia had grown up to become the mother of "Little Miss Tiny Colorado," one of JonBenet's numerous titles. The caretaker Nedra also saw another beauty in the wings and pressed for pageant competitions for the next generation of beauty titles.

Contrary to what Patsy Ramsey may have said among her social group and the beauty pageant glimpses the press exposed after her death, JonBenet did not relish the spotlight or the competition. Her childhood friend, Lindsey Phillips, who

Prostitution of Justice

was the same age as Burke and a few years older than JonBenet, knew the little beauty princess did not embrace the beauty pageant industry with the passion of Nedra, Patsy, and Pam Paugh. Rehearsals, voice and dance coaching, costume fittings, and weekend competitions left little time to be a little girl instead of a Barbie Doll.

Judith Phillips, Lindsey's mother, and a family friend from Atlanta who had moved to Boulder a few years earlier, helped the Ramseys find their mansion on 15th Street and settle in Boulder. Patsy and Judith shared their pregnancy experiences in Atlanta. In 1987, Patsy gave birth to Burke on January 27, and one month later, on February 27, Judith gave birth to her second child, Lindsey. Upon moving to Boulder, Judith began a photography business while her husband, Robert, attended the University of Colorado Law School. Judith's work won contests, and her portraiture work blossomed. Patsy understood from childhood the power of images and the use of media. She loved Judith's work, and their bond grew.

During Patsy's cancer treatments, Colorado Woman's News published a feature on Patsy Ramsey in her truly heroic struggle against ovarian cancer. The magazine published Judith Phillips' images, capturing a mother and daughter-like soul as JonBenet, in a striped t-shirt with her dirty blonde hair in a pageboy, kissed the back of her mother's bald head. Showing the power of faith, one closeup shows Patsy with the head of an ornate cross lightly clenched in her teeth.

Prostitution of Justice

From there, the relationship only grew, as did the business interests of John Ramsey and Robert Phillips. Standing nearly six feet, six inches with a broad face, Phillips had all but taken doctorates in accounting and computer science before deciding to enter law school at CU. The socially awkward new lawyer graduated second in his law school class. John and Robert had known each other from the days of Hayes Microcomputers. Phillips sold his interest in the Atlanta company to pursue his new career in law in the Rocky Mountains.

Patsy visited Boulder in anticipation of moving to the sweet, snug, safe city when John decided to move his business north to the picturesque town. John hired Robert Phillips to work on his estate planning as Phillips moved from divorce work to trusts and estates. Patsy invited the Phillips to her charities and parties. At the 1994 Christmas party, four-year-old JonBenet descended the grand staircase wearing a red sequined, sparkling pageant dress with a sophisticated model's grace. Her hair was bleached Marilyn Monroe blonde. Everyone stared at the transformation from a tomboy into a dazzling four-year-old Beauty Princess.

Aside from the stunning glamour, JonBenet voiced her feelings about her trophies from children's beauty pageants to Lindsey Phillips. While visiting JonBenet one day, Lindsey couldn't help but notice the pageant trophies in JonBenet's bedroom. "They're not really mine; they're more my mom's trophies," JonBenet said.

Later, Lindsey, saddened by JonBenet's death, explained the little beauty princess's sinking enthusiasm for pageants to her mother. Judith had earlier noticed JonBenet's southern-styled big blond hair when Patsy and family returned to Boulder from their summer home in Charlevoix, Michigan. Judith asked Patsy why she dyed JonBenet's hair. "It was the hot summer sun in Charlevoix," Patsy said.

To the eye of the professional photographer who had photographed Patsy, JonBenet, and Burke over the years, who had worked with numerous models sporting both natural and artificially colored hair, Patsy's sunlight claim sounded disingenuous. Judith simply shrugged her shoulders and attributed this to Patsy's upbringing in the South.

Did Patsy Ramsey's normal maternal expressions of love revolve around JonBenet's future as a woman or as a sex object by putting the four-year-old in satin hot pants and bleaching her hair blonde? Did Patsy lie to Judith about JonBenet's hair because she found something socially unacceptable about the applications of artificial "beauty" inside their home to a supposedly perfect child? Did her lie suggest denial or embarrassment for wanting to make her child more beautiful, more competitive, more fetching?

Prostitution of Justice

Patsy had long fancied herself an artist and so certainly would have appreciated the "art" in the staging of her daughter's death were it not so freakishly personal. She might have recognized the method of the garrote as one described in a book police found on her nightstand during the search of the mansion, a spy novel by Alan Folsom entitled The Day After Tomorrow. Folsom's thriller includes not only the use of a garrote but multiple beheadings.[7]

The movie Ransom may have suggested to the intruder/writer that the bagman would be "screened for electronic devices" and that the kidnapper was "familiar with police procedures." Patsy watched Ransom with the Whites at their Christmas party the night before the murder. The uncanny plagiarism of the movie in the ransom note and suggestive beheading in the thriller on the bedside table parallel what happened to the corpse in the cellar as it suffered a virtual "beheading" by a garrote.

With their obvious sentimentality for Christmas and envisioning JonBenet as an angel, John and Patsy ordered the inscription on JonBenet's headstone in Atlanta with a small angel at the top. It describes her short life as ending on December 25, 1996, although the autopsy report insists on a time of death after midnight, between one and two in the morning on December 26.

Prostitution of Justice

Chapter Six: "We Know Who You Are"

On October 13, 1999, a beefy man with a hound dog's face and thick glasses took the podium for a press conference to report on the Boulder County Grand Jury's deliberations and decision 34 months after JonBenet's murder. District Attorney Alex Hunter appeared like a plump Don Quixote. During a press conference in the first week after the murder, he once said to the press, "We know who you are," and that soon, with appropriate bluster, the killer would be caught. Of course, he offered his role as the braggadocio long before Ramsey's press agents and a massively published intruder theory soured his claim.

No matter his assertions, Hunter, a windmill himself as a career politician in his seventh elected term as Boulder County District Attorney, had only bluffed. He had no trial attorneys, only Assistant D.A.s skilled in plea bargains. He had no one in his office who could tilt with a cyclone: the law firm of Haddon, Morgan, and Foreman.

Hunter's office used plea bargains for nearly 28 years to imitate justice, rarely developing his staff's skills through trial work to build competency in a courtroom to face the talent of Ramsey's defense team. He also didn't have the political power Hal Haddon commanded from Colorado to Washington D.C. Beyond his legal expertise inside and outside of the courtroom,

Prostitution of Justice

Hal Haddon had become a Godfather of Politics, masterminding campaigns, developing legislation, often working as a campaign manager for the likes of Robert Kennedy before his assassination and in Gary Hart's failed national presidential campaign that sank in a sex scandal. Alex Hunter worked alongside Haddon in politics as Boulder presented a Democratic stronghold in Colorado. The governor of Colorado, Roy Romer, along with state and federal congressmen and senators, were also beholden to Hal Haddon for his work on their campaigns, strategy, and legislation. Haddon's firm had even handled tax issues for Bill and Hillary Clinton.

The Ramseys' wealth had mustered a world-class team of super lawyers to fight a formal accusation, charges, or a trial. Alex Hunter did not have the talent, the stomach, or even sufficient funds in the county's coffers to fight Haddon, Morgan, and Foreman, nor was he prepared for the ridicule he would suffer once the Ramseys were charged and then acquitted. His prosecutors could never make competent use of incompetently gathered evidence.

Hunter's office began to fumble the case in the first hours before John carried JonBenet's body up the stairs. His D.A.'s office did not initially bother to send anyone to the chaotic crime scene. With a smattering of legal guidance, the innumerable errors in search, witnesses, and evidence gathering

Prostitution of Justice

may have been preserved, at least providing a smattering of competence, perhaps collecting enough evidence to try the case.

Criminal charges, such as child abuse resulting in death, don't just pop out of a hat. The officer needs to see, smell, taste, touch, read, or hear something that would give a reasonable person the belief that a crime has been committed and the defendant committed it. Once that threshold of a reasonable belief is established, probable cause exists. Once the officer has that "probable cause," he can arrest the defendant(s).

The defendant isn't guilty beyond a reasonable doubt at that point. The person accused can plead not guilty and go to trial to fight the charges. The state has the burden of proof, a very high burden of "proof beyond a reasonable doubt." Every citizen is entitled to a lawyer, but if the citizen is wealthy, the citizen can also have expensive experts who can raise doubt. If employed, the hired expert may introduce scientific evidence to raise questions, depleting the prosecution of its reasonable doubt. Universally, the citizen can admit guilt and, with less expense than claiming innocence, plead guilty to a lesser charge and have some charges dropped or fixed. Plea bargains are cheaper and easier. They are so common that criminal trials occur rarely. Those lawyers who try cases successfully receive notoriety and better fees for facing and winning over juries.

Probable cause is defined by the courts. It means that the total facts and circumstances create a degree of certainty in a reasonable and prudent person that a crime has been committed and that the suspect committed it. Colorado Revised Statutes define the term:

1. A peace officer may arrest a person when: ... 3) He has probable cause to believe that an offense has been committed and has probable cause to believe that the offense was committed by the person to be arrested.[8]

Determining probable cause is not equivalent to brain surgery and does not require three years of legal training. Cops do it every day in domestic violence matters, driving under the influence, or for speeding tickets. In fact, the common occurrence of police officers finding probable cause and arresting a suspect contributed greatly to the bureaucratic infighting between the Boulder Police and the Boulder District Attorney. The D.A.'s office claimed insufficient probable cause in the Ramsey case. The cops, stunned and embarrassed by the feckless direction of the case, began crawling into bureaucratic bunkers and trenches or leaving the department when the causes they found lay bludgeoned in a bureaucracy.

Commander John Eller was removed from the case in 1997 and announced his retirement immediately thereafter. Chief Tom Kolby of the Boulder P.D. read the political pulse of the community as the investigation stagnated. The top police brass had the microphone and reported ongoing failure to develop sufficient evidence to arrest anyone in the now internationally infamous and botched investigation. Kolby resigned in 1998.

Prostitution of Justice

Linda Arndt, the hapless detective assigned to monitor the crime scene and its house full of witnesses and potential suspects, whom Boulder authorities blamed for all things done unprofessionally by Boulder P.D., sued for the scapegoating in a Federal defamation action in 1998. She resigned the following year. Her case was dismissed during jury deliberations. Detective Steve Thomas, a 13-year career police officer and the lead investigator for 20 months, resigned from the Boulder Police Department, disgusted at the turn of the investigation to an intruder theory. He published JonBenet: Inside the Ramsey Murder Investigation, and John and Patsy sued him. Thomas claims he never paid the Ramseys a "dime."

Fleet White became a former friend of the Ramseys. He supported Steve Thomas and his theory that John and Patsy Ramsey had murdered their daughter. Thomas and White believed the couple covered up the crime with a fake kidnapping.

A headshot of Fleet White from a family photo session in 1995 reveals a supremely confident man. In an open white shirt, his fingers clasped behind his head, his blue eyes steady but warm, Fleet White presents a John Wayne grin and clean-shaven face. A small cleft in his chin adds to that picture of strength. That was before his hair silvered and before John Ramsey fingered him for the murder of JonBenet.

Although Boulder P.D. cleared White as a suspect, as did D.A. Alex Hunter, John Ramsey's assertions stuck with

Prostitution of Justice

internet gossip. Years later, the next Boulder D.A., Mary Keenan Lacy, would also clear the Whites as suspects. While she was at it, the D.A. also cleared the Ramseys, in endorsement of the intruder theory. Nevertheless, internet media claimed White was a suspect, and no amount of official exoneration would fully exonerate him, or his family, of their public burden.

Fleet White grew up in California, the son of an oil and minerals magnate, and continued in the family business. He relocated to Boulder with his wife, Priscilla, and two children. They attended St. John's Episcopal Church, as did the Ramseys. They were also present for the orchestrated "Christian Innocence" photo op arranged by public relations expert Pat Korton. Understanding the value and power of the press, the politically well-connected law firm of Haddon, Morgan, and Foreman had retained Korton for the Ramseys. The Whites had been snagged into sharing their Christian values and beliefs with the Ramseys by association. Later, a belief in their friends' involvement in the calculated, brutal murder of JonBenet emerged, a view nearly impossible to accept for the Whites before JonBenet's funeral in Atlanta, Georgia.

John Ramsey, with his high-power connections in Atlanta and the runaway news media in the chase, could arrange for the CNN interview on January 1, 1997. Fleet White thought it cheap theatrics and did not think Patsy should appear on nationwide TV in the state of sedative narcosis he had witnessed. White grew increasingly uncomfortable and increasingly disheartened by the Southern ostentation he observed while with the family and friends in their Southern society. He did not appreciate Atlanta's leisure class, where servants attended to any need. He and Priscilla left the accommodation arranged with John Ramsey's son for a motel room.

The situation had grown heated. The Whites had been lodged with John Ramsey's son by his first marriage until they argued, vehemently, and Atlanta police were called to quell the disturbance. Fleet White had become increasingly suspicious as to why John and Patsy Ramsey refused to cooperate with the police. He saw them using lawyers like a bomb shelter, all while raising their Boulder tragedy into an international event through the hysterical CNN broadcast.

The funeral for JonBenet Ramsey did not go as peacefully or memorialize the reverence her death merited. The feud between the Whites and the Ramseys spattered like hot grease over the orchestrated innocence of the social event John and Patsy had made of their grief. Fleet White reportedly became so unhinged in his sense of injustice and what he thought was feigned innocence that he created a scene in Ramsey's view. The Whites did not return to Boulder in John's private jet with other friends who had attended the funeral. In fact, that "Come to Jesus" moment between John Ramsey and Fleet White riveted the accusations of wrongdoing against both

Prostitution of Justice

the gentlemen and some mysterious intruder for the rest of the 20th century.

Three months after the funeral, the investigation into the murder in Boulder, Colorado, of JonBenet Ramsey, Little Miss Christmas, had taken the international mystery and freak show to a hyper-inflated tabloid food fight for advertising paydays. To lubricate the presses, publishers, and journalists of all varieties, so vilified at the St. John's Memorial Service, proceeded to crack the case with fistfuls of dollars and, more glorious than gold, a few minutes of fame. They interviewed neighbors and witnesses, bought and sold private information, and traded for insider leaks like fishmongers. Next, tabloids charged in with lurid photographs and headlines in red ink: "Santa Claus Did It! Mom Did It! Where Was Burke!"

Ramsey's law firm cried out against a "Rush to Judgment" and, reasonably enough in their client's best interests, demanded that authorities explore the crime to identify the intruder who targeted JonBenet Ramsey. They argued that the narrow focus on John and Patsy ignored the long list of other possible suspects the law firm's investigators and the press had now reported. This did not give up reasonable doubt. Instead, the press unctuously milked unrelated incidents, cracking the case for the public in a money-buttered frying pan of headlines, blistering the yoke of all those accused, those hounded, arrested, and jailed, their lives all left as broken shells.

Prostitution of Justice

Almost a year after the JonBenet tragedy began, on December 21, 1997, Susannah Chase, a University of Colorado student, was murdered, and the killer smeared her blood for a block over a downtown alley. She died hideously, terrified, and forgotten. Almost a decade later, the semen of Diego Almos Alcalde, which he had left on her clothing, was brought to justice in 2008.

A hungry press, dissatisfied with progress in the JonBenet Ramsey case, noted Chase's death with more a rebuke of the D.A. and Boulder P.D. than news coverage of a murder victim. The routine mission of a cop or a D.A. to find enough reasonable doubt to charge the Ramseys settled like a thunderstorm over the Rockies, deluging the Boulder P.D., the D.A.'s office, and Alex Hunter, personally, with demands for an arrest or resignation, reasonable doubt be damned.

The case had stalled. The police had made arrests, a private eye, and a photo lab technician, but only after the Boulder P.D. itself had fumbled the autopsy photographs of JonBenet Ramsey to the *Globe*, a tabloid magazine out of Boca Raton, Florida. Despite all their efforts, the police had no suspects outside of the parents.

The scenic city at the base of the Rocky Mountains had never seen such worldwide attention, and the affluent and publicly vocal citizenry did not like it. The D.A.'s office allowed the police to be flummoxed within days after the Ramseys lawyered up for their failure to find probable cause for

Prostitution of Justice

an arrest of the parents. Hunter knew he would be the victim in the courtroom once in the jaws of Haddon's trial lawyers. Even worse, Alex Hunter was compromised. To accomplish seven terms as Boulder's District Attorney, Alex Hunter knew a lot of people. Most importantly, he knew Hal Haddon, the Godfather of Colorado's Democratic Party and a man Hunter knew better than to cross. The District Attorney had talked, blathered, and boasted that the murderer would be arrested and prosecuted. But it didn't happen, and Hunter knew it wouldn't happen outside of a confession or a miracle.

Chapter Seven: A Legendary Theory

Three months after JonBenet's murder, DA Alex Hunter found a man with the credentials and determination to lead the Ramseys out of the forest and create an alternative suspect with his intruder theory. Enter a legend: Lou Smit, a smallish, white-haired, retired career cop from the Pueblo County Sheriff's Office 140 miles south of Boulder. When he entered law enforcement, he believed the work to be a calling from God. Smit barely reached the physical height regulation at 5'9" in 1966 when he joined the Sheriff's Office. Whatever he lacked in size, he did not lack in respect through the decades. He had solved gritty murders, many of them, with a counterintuitive knack that had amazed his colleagues and the criminals arrested, tried, and convicted. His national reputation grew when he solved the murder of Karen Grammar, sister of Hollywood star Kelsey Grammar. In 1991, he also arrested serial killer Robert Charles Browne, who claimed to have committed 48 homicides, none of which were confirmed.

Smit retired in 1996. He bragged that he "had never lost a homicide case" out of 200 cases where a suspect had been arrested and tried. He could have added to that claim that he won a homicide case that was never charged with his "Intruder Theory" in the Ramsey case. His long career in law enforcement had also caused him to work with grand juries at the time when Hal Haddon was establishing his career in criminal defense.

Early on during Lou Smit's police career, the Colorado Public Defenders Office came into existence in 1970 under the direction of Rollie Rogers, a colorful criminal defense lawyer. Rogers hired young Hal Haddon as the first Chief Trial Deputy or that office. The Public Defenders Office opened with four statewide locations, one of which was in Pueblo, Colorado, where Hal Haddon and Lou Smit would get to know each other from opposite sides of the courtroom. When Alex Hunter agreed to seek an independent outside investigator to examine the murder of JonBenet Ramsey, the Ramsey defense team would know more than the average bear about the investigator, Lou Smit, all the way down to his religious fervor. For Alex Hunter, hiring a special investigator relieved the unrelenting public pressure on him and his office.

The early accusations rising from the public centered on John and Patsy, with much of the press leading that public opinion with its saturation reporting. Simultaneously, the public relations team employed by the Ramseys painted the parents as bereaved innocents while heaping disdain on the media. The success of that public relations campaign gave breathing space to the parents. It also gave time for their defense team to continue its forced march through the swamp of accusations to seek evidence of other suspects while scripting a new narrative.

Prostitution of Justice

As a special investigator, Lou Smit, the old pro, acknowledged what he had already concluded about the author of the ransom note. In the first meeting, Smit said, "Look, I don't know if you're going to hire me, but I'll give you a freebie. Whoever wrote this note did not do it after the murder."[9]

To Lou Smit's knowledge, a man who had studied murder and knew murderers throughout his lifelong professional experience, his instincts validated his hypothesis to fit a single intruder and perpetrator from within the scope of his experience. That free advice could only come from the gut, not from any provable facts. That theory ran counter to the established position of handwriting experts, who believed that Patsy Ramsey had written the ransom note while John had acted in other areas as a separate co-conspirator. As the "freebie" ignored Patsy Ramsey's handwriting in the note, Smit's assumption could presuppose a single actor in the crime, one who enters, kills, and writes the ransom note. To his credit, by the time Smit had entered the case, John and Patsy Ramsey had been smeared from hell to breakfast as fiends in a monstrous coverup. Smit didn't jump to that initial conclusion. On the other hand, he discredited enough of the totality of evidence that did not point to an intruder to provide swamp creatures in law and politics with a pass on a criminal prosecution.

To get a feel for the investigation, Smit was one day parked at the curb outside the abandoned mansion on 15th Street. In a moment of divine intervention, John and Patsy

Prostitution of Justice

Ramsey drove up to their now-vacant home. The press had treated the couple notoriously for stonewalling investigators under the "advice of counsel." Yet, when Smit introduced himself, they agreed to pray with the detective. And, at that moment, they bonded as Christians often do in an affirmation of their shared faith. Smit later stated that he had put a lot of Christians in prison, and even if friendly with the couple, he would do the same to these parents if that is where the evidence took him. Nevertheless, the couple's sincerity and faith had touched him so powerfully that he would become a fervent, if not evangelical, defender in the grand jury investigation.

In his trademark manner, Smit questioned the conventional wisdom and looked for alternative suspects. In time, he postulated that an intruder brought a stun gun, the tape, and the rope into the Ramsey home. The suspect then wrote the note while waiting for the family to return from the White's Christmas party. Smit based his intruder theory on the apparent absence of motive in John and Patsy's life stories: no histories of abuse or negligence, no criminal records, no rumors of substance abuse, no financial problems. Smit only found devoted parents and good Christians in the community.

Since neither John nor Patsy had a history of arrests or gossip about abusing their children sexually or physically, Smit surmised no motive existed to commit a ritual-like murder and cover it up. For Smit, Steve Thomas' theory that Patsy murdered her child in a rage over a bed-soiling incident is like "pulling a motive out of the air."[10] He insists that whoever committed the murder must have been a person who thinks and acts like a criminal. Given the results, whoever committed the crimes certainly thought and acted like a criminal, or criminals, for some time at the Ramsey household Christmas Night.

For a career police officer to believe that those who victimize children act in a certain way in public or are not found to have acted in a suspicious way in public records places his theories on a treadmill. To assume that perpetrators show their disaffection to victims in public, never escalate maltreatment, and never respond to jealousy with violence reveals a psychological and statistical blind spot the size of a planet as regards the nature of murder and violence. Had interrogators separated and interviewed John, Patsy, and Burke, a motive may have surfaced: precipitous rage, fear, jealousy, intoxicated revenge, frustration over spilled pineapple, bedwetting, or pedophilia, perhaps even volatile sibling rivalry. No one will ever know what such interviews would have unearthed.

Smit states that JonBenet was a "pedophile's dream." He ignores who made her that way. That John married a former Miss West Virginia and let his trophy wife, in turn, groom their daughter as a sexually nuanced exhibitionist doesn't bespeak a Christian sense of modesty. Further, if JonBenet protested about her involvement while her mother insisted on dressing her up in sexualized clothing, forcing her to wear makeup and color her hair, and making her dance and sing for an audience, what's

Prostitution of Justice

the difference in Patsy's mind between a child and a doll? Through all the attention Patsy showered on JonBenet, how did Burke feel?

Because no footprints were found in the dusting of snow from the night before, Smit claimed that the "intruder" left no footprints in the snow outside the home. That is because snow melts, and none of the dusting remains by late morning for forensic photographs. Smit does not explain why no shoe print, or even a suggestion of one, appeared in the moist earth. He finds evidence of an intrusion at the basement room window, which John admitted he had broken himself when he lost his house keys. Never mind that cobwebs blocked the window and lay undisturbed at the time the police inspected the basement. The window also lay under a grate that would render it nearly invisible to an intruder(s).

Smit didn't see footprints or cobwebs in the crime scene photographs. Two separate entomologists examined enlarged photographs of the window, grate, and webbing. Both experts identified spider webs in place. Smit refused to accept an earlier police examination that found the window "undisturbed." A locksmith examining pry marks on the doors (requested by John Ramsey) failed to find any evidence of a forced entry. No hair, fiber evidence, or fingerprints were found on the broken window to the basement. The basement window was not so small that Smit, in his investigation, could not climb through it to gain entry. It remained small enough that Smit or a child would have trouble squeezing through that opening and not leave a thread, a fiber, a footprint, a clue, or a breach of the cobwebs strung there.

Smit places much emphasis on a suitcase below the window. Could an intruder have used that suitcase as a step to crawl down into the basement? Probably not, as Fleet White recalls placing the suitcase below the window while he searched the house early that morning with John.[11] Smit ignores the facts that disturb his theory. He disregards the suitcase, melting snow, and visible spider webs for an invisible stun gun, Patsy's and Burke's fingerprints on the pineapple bowl, and a failed search for a forced entry. Smit ignores a departure by the same basement window where entry was gained. Yet, there lies the dead girl, so very near the exit. And there remains a ransom note, written by Patsy Ramsey, on the stairway leading to the second floor while abandoning that $118,000 body for ransom?

Would an intruder smart enough to leave no physical trace and ethereal enough to pass through unopened doors and windows be stupid enough to forget to take the tortured body of the child? Smart or stupid, could the intruder not have realized that the body, sooner or later, would be found with or without the diversion of the ransom note? And why did the intruder(s) want the body to be found bludgeoned, bound, molested, and strangled, yet dressed and covered with a blanket? Respect for a child's modesty, even in death, occurs in parents, not in murderous fiends.

Prostitution of Justice

Smit stressed the presence of a footprint from a Hi-Tec shoe near the spot in the basement where John found his daughter's body. This never proved the presence of an intruder, as Smit suggested. It proved there was a footprint—a footprint made by none other than Burke Ramsey in the room Patsy used for hiding Christmas presents because she didn't think the children entered it. A mysterious palm print on the door to the room where JonBenet's body was found turned out to belong to Patsy. The pubic hair found on the blanket wrapped around JonBenet's corpse wasn't pubic hair but simply hair from Patsy.

Smit also introduced an invisible stun gun to his intruder theory, one never uncovered in the search, and claimed that whoever killed JonBenet subdued her with a stun gun. Months later, he tested his theory on live pigs. Though the marks did not match precisely, Smit surmised that the device caused the small abrasions on JonBenet's neck. The child's unconsciousness, he argued, explains the deadly quiet accomplished by JonBenet's murderer and stealthy non-abduction. Unfortunately for that theory, the manufacturer of the stun gun discredited it because it marketed no product that would make marks on JonBenet's body consistent with the design of their product.

Lawrence Schiller, in his book *Perfect Murder, Perfect Town* (later produced as a made-for-TV movie), raised Smit to the status of folk hero for his unrelenting insistence on the intruder and stun-gun theory.[12] The made-for-TV movie stars Kris Kristofferson as Smit. Although the intruder theory provided the Ramseys and their attorneys with "reasonable doubt" for their public relations purposes and may have convinced a jury had the Ramseys gone to trial, it did not provide any physical evidence to contradict the much more substantial "probable cause" the grand jury had been assigned to find, and did find.

Smit asserted that the perpetrator could not have written the ransom note after the murder. This was an opinion, not evidence. No matter when the note was written, the note itself is evidence, and few would disagree that whoever wrote it was involved in the staging of the crime scene, if not the murder itself. After a decade of speculation, investigation, innumerable witness interviews, accusations, rumors, and "targets," no credible physical or eyewitness evidence of an intruder ever materialized.

In the 21st Century, DNA has replaced much of the guesswork in police investigations. Once CSI collects the perpetrator's DNA at the crime scene and identifies who left the mystery specimen, viewers can tune in next week for a new episode. The story grows more complex outside of Hollywood when the DNA recovered is less than minuscule and requires partial destruction to identify. Advances in DNA be damned. It requires a spec more than what is available to draw a conclusion.

Prostitution of Justice

The foreign DNA under JonBenet's fingernails and on her panties that Smit insists must have come from the intruder was identified as having come from two different sources. The first sample recovered is so slight and degraded that it remains virtually useless as evidence. The deposit could have been days, weeks, or months old. It could have been a trace from a kid's party. Dr. Henry C. Lee of the Henry C. Lee Institute of Forensic Sciences at the University of New Haven tracked down such DNA samples in panties like JonBenet wore that were mass-produced in Thailand. A spec of foreign DNA was found under JonBenet's fingernails, so slight that the coroner's office reinspected scissors used to harvest the specimen looking for its origin. The existence of foreign DNA from a thrice-removed corpse, unsecured crime scene, and throngs of human mingling exists only as a vague reference to the magical evidence of DNA. In this case, there just wasn't enough magical DNA to identify anyone for anything.

Nevertheless, the debate rages on. "New advances in DNA technology" now provide a Holy Grail to identify a suspect. So, what if it doesn't? What if the DNA sample is still too insignificant even for new technology? What if the new technology doesn't identify a new suspect? Could the "advance" in technology only be a red herring? Could it be that there are no other suspects outside of the family?

Meanwhile, the ransom note, the smoking gun of the JonBenet murder investigation, survived as the number one

Prostitution of Justice

source for probable cause to have arrested Patsy Ramsey and John as co-conspirators for Child Abuse Resulting in Death. Where is it now? It lies hidden away in the Boulder District Attorney's archives, never to be seen by experts again and of no matter to the dead.

At one point, the press reported that even the CBI could not identify the disguised handwriting as that of Patsy. That misstated the facts. In fact, this is an outright lie. When the writer of a ransom note disguises the handwriting, say, by using the left hand instead of the dominant right hand, positive identification is disguised, not eliminated, by the deception. Can we positively identify Clayton Moore as the Lone Ranger while he wears his disguise? No, the mask hides a major identification factor, the skull casing of the eyes, at a glance. Nevertheless, we can tell the shape of the head, face, nose, lips, and jaw, the skin, eyes, and hair color. We can identify the voice, the nuances of speech patterns, and accents. And, when placing a photograph of Clayton Moore next to one of the Lone Ranger, we can identify with some degree of certainty Clayton Moore and positively not Bozo the Clown. Since we deal with the reality of a ransom note used to cover up an unimaginable monstrosity and not a television fiction requiring a suspension of belief, we must trust senses, reason, and the real over the invisible. But the original note is unavailable.

Early on, the CBI position was that Patsy Ramsey possibly, but not definitely, wrote the ransom note. Meanwhile, those handwriting experts from the law enforcement community involved in the murder investigation had positively eliminated every suspect but Patsy. More factually relevant, when the CBI administered the fourth of five handwriting samples on April 12, 1997, and requested that Patsy write a copy of the ransom note with her left hand, authorities could not eliminate Patsy as the author of the note. Some of Patsy's letters and numbers were mirror images of those found in the ransom note.[13]

What has not gained enough attention regarding the ransom note's author is that Patsy was ambidextrous. As we learned, when Patsy and Judith Phillips played softball for the team John Ramsey's business sponsored, both Patsy and Judith Phillips could catch or throw with either hand. That left or right-handed skill of Patsy Ramsey appears in the ransom note.

In 1984, Darnay Hoffman made a name for himself by representing and defending the New York City Subway Vigilante Bernard Goetz. A handsome man and a staunch defender of the poor and the sub rosa entrepreneurs of society, such as the Mayflower Madam of New York City, whom he married, Hoffman employed three independent handwriting experts: David Liebman, Cina L. Wong, and the author in the spring of 1997. All three independently concluded, without consulting each other, that Patsy Ramsey had written the note. Their analyses are contained in sworn statements filed in the

Prostitution of Justice

Boulder District Court, which have appeared on internet websites devoted to the JonBenet Ramsey crime. A great curiosity for the untrained eye arises in the change in the handwriting as the note progresses from somewhat crudely drawn characters to more substantially well-formed letter structures. Peter Boyles, a Denver talk show host who enthusiastically skewered Boulder law enforcement, commented on this and concluded on his radio program that the writer switched hands in mid-letter. In fact, an ambidextrous person, such as Patsy, can quickly establish new muscle memory and adapt to the change in handedness. Somebody in the house made the practice note found in the kitchen, and according to many amateur and professional handwriting experts, Patsy Ramsey wrote the note to a reasonable degree of scientific certainty.

According to John Ramsey in their New York Times bestseller, The Death of Innocence, their attorneys employed credentialed document examiners to compare their clients' handwriting to that of the note."[14] The Ramseys' own hired experts, though they eliminated John, could not eliminate Patsy. Not surprisingly, these privately hired, anonymous experts suggested that there had been only a very low probability that Patsy wrote the note. Even less surprisingly, their written reports have never been released to the public. They lay hidden behind confidentiality and publishing agreements held by John alone since Patsy's death. Without these reports, other

Prostitution of Justice

handwriting experts can never review the work of Ramsey's experts nor refute or confirm what features in the ransom note and what specific specimens of Patsy's handwriting they relied upon in reaching their opinions.

Given his reputation for detail, Smit's denial of alternative possibilities from the time when the ransom note was written, when the ransom note was the most important piece of evidence in the case, put Smit in a position to undermine confidence in the Boulder Police Department's work. Smit began his reexamination of the evidence as an outsider. Despite the lenses of his experience, or perhaps because of it, he placed enormous emphasis on hunches and faith, stretching stubborn facts like elastic to fit his thesis. Smit worked the case on the assumption that one person, a single intruder, committed the murder. He denied or disregarded the possibility of two persons being involved in the crime: one who killed, the other who wrote the note. His viewpoint and dogged determination to find a single, ghostlike alternative suspect haunted his investigation all the way to the grand jury and will haunt the case forever.

Chapter Eight: Invisible Evidence

Forgery is the world's oldest form of identity theft. From paper and pen to the art of handwriting, fortunes have been stolen. In response, experts have studied, investigated, and offered their opinions as to the authenticity of documents for centuries. That explains why courts and juries prefer the opinions of forensic experts over squabbling inheritors, dishonest merchants, or a bamboozling land grabber. While stereoscopic microscopes and ultraviolet light have technologically improved document examination as a forensic science, so have breakthroughs in psychology as a tool of advanced methods of criminal investigation. The famous FBI profilers borrow from psychiatry, forensic psychology, and criminology. These new horizons in the investigation were explored in relation to the psychological profile and the underlying personality characteristics of Patsy Ramsey's word choice.

A psychiatrist, Dr. Andrew G. Hodges, had worked on the O.J. Simpson case with the FBI, extending his knowledge of psycholinguistics into the field of forensic investigation. He became aware of JonBenet's murder in the same way as millions of others. He read about it in the newspapers, saw replays on television of the six-year-old's sexualized appearances in beauty pageants, and learned each new detail from those same sources every day into the night, and then from that newcomer to public information, the internet.

Once the publication of the ransom note finally occurred, Dr. Hodges read it and applied his new science of linguistic profiling to the evidence. To digest his linguistic theories into enormously simplistic terms, psycholinguistics is the psychological analysis of phrasing, word choice, and echoes within the juxtaposition of ideas, words, and syntactical patterns arising from within the unconscious mind. Applying his science, Dr. Hodges determined the ransom note amounted to a confession by Patsy Ramsey to the crimes against JonBenet.[15]

For example, the note begins with "Listen carefully!" Dr. Hodges finds the tone controlling, with the urgency of control continuing through the duration of the note. The writer fears losing power over the usual rank-and-file order within the writer's dominion, while other words such as "Listen" carry powerful underlying emotional triggers related to cancer and Patsy's feminine image and decline.[16]

A dissonance arises in Patsy's inner conflicts between her declining sexuality and JonBenet's premature budding into the new beauty contestant, the challenger to her mother's fading glory. Dr. Andrew G. Hodges, psychiatrist and prolific author, found subconscious clues in the ransom note. He believed that Patsy's personal despair with cancer resonated within the ransom note. The new beauty contestant had replaced Patsy. Dr.

Hodges hypothesized that the inconsistencies between Patsy's lost glamour and her female child lead to a symbolic beheading, as the ransom note suggests, and the strangulation also identifies her as the author. Obviously, the writer would not consciously intend to embed extraordinary underlying messages about the author's own psyche at the time of the writing, and there lies the importance and value of a psycholinguistics expert.

Dr. Hodges contacted one of his sources in the FBI. The agent referred him to Boulder Police Chief Mark Beckner. Dr. Hodges offered the Boulder Chief of Police a summary of the results of his analysis on December 5, 1997. Beckner listened politely and then declined to consider Dr. Hodges' work. Taken aback by the lack of interest or even curiosity, Dr. Hodges persisted with his theory. Eventually, he even tried to submit his work to the grand jury.

Had Alex Hunter allowed psycholinguist Dr. Hodges and his research associates to testify to the grand jury as to their analysis of the ransom note, the subliminal confession would likely have added to the probable cause that the grand jurors found for their eventual indictment. However, Hunter knew no formal accusation would be lodged against the Ramseys. He knew he would not be signing one. The less damning evidence presented, the better.

Dr. Hodges presented a theory as invisible as an intruder, but his postmortem psychological autopsy of Patsy

Prostitution of Justice

Ramsey and the crime scene does describe a formidable argument for Patsy's motive and involvement in killing JonBenet. Hodges believed the murderer or murderers intended to throw dust in the eyes of the police by staging a kidnapping. The ransom note, this crucial piece of evidence, was left by the perpetrator(s) to confuse the investigation, as it was surely meant to do, but lay hidden from the public from the day after Christmas 1996 until September 7, 1997, when it was published in Newsweek.

Ignored by authorities, Dr. Hodges presented his evidence to the public while the case languished in the hands of the Boulder County Grand Jury. In his first book on the murder, *A Mother Gone Bad*, Dr. Hodges states that Patsy Ramsey wrote the note and that she wrote it immediately after the murder.[17] He later establishes Patsy's likely mental condition through interviews with her associates, other writings of hers, and her own public statements. He also identifies the psychological profile derived from the ransom note to the various psychological roots of her southern upbringing and Miss West Virginia title and brings this forward to the traumas of ovarian cancer, loss of image, sexuality, and jealousy of JonBenet's success. He looks at the way the little girl was murdered and filters it through the images of Patsy's own emotional and physical losses and rejection. The note's fantastic length and laughably low ransom demand give clues to the writer's interest in something other than an efficient and profitable kidnapping.

This refusal of assistance originating from outside the Boulder Police Department became a hallmark of the Ramsey murder investigation. As noted, detectives from the Denver Police Department offered their expertise in the early moments of the discovery of the kidnapping on the morning of December 26, 1996. No thanks. Bill Hagmaier from the FBI's National Center for the Analysis of Violent Crimes received that same lack of interest in his profile.

When Dr. Andrew Hodges, a respected psychiatrist who produced a monograph on the bogus ransom note and identified Patsy as its author, offered to testify to the grand jury, he was ignored. Detective Steve Thomas resigned from the investigation in August of 1998, disgusted by the DA's office, and did not testify.[18] Most incredibly, only Burke Ramsey testified, although the power of the grand jury subpoena could have forced John and Patsy's testimony. Wouldn't that have been interesting, or at least of interest, to the jurors?

Despite international interest, evidence, such as the ransom note, remains hidden. The members of the grand jury, forbidden by law to speak, issued no report, and the door closed to a prosecution of the leading suspects in the death of JonBenet. Burke Ramsey never faced legal jeopardy. At just under ten years of age immediately prior to his sister's murder, Colorado law would prohibit charging Burke, as criminal statutes prohibited finding him competent to have been charged with a crime while under the age of ten.

The tortured path of justice in Boulder had its elements of dark humor. Denver radio talk show host Peter Boyles often opened his morning talk show with a musical cut from Warner Brothers' "Looney Tunes" and invited discussion of the Boulder Police Department's investigation and the District Attorney's Office, and repeatedly called for the release of the ransom note. Boulder's reputation as a college playground for grey-haired hippies and leftist politics allowed musings as to which "small foreign faction" was at work in the Ramsey household.

Evidence in a grand jury comes in part by subpoenaed testimony. Retired cop Lou Smit, defender of the Ramseys, through his worldwide circulation of the Intruder Theory, demanded that he be allowed to testify. That was not Smit's call. The District Attorney determines witnesses. Yet, with powerful legal assistance and no lack of faith, Smit forced the issue through a petition to the court, arguing he must present his investigation's results. In Colorado, witness selection and testimony belong to the D.A.'s office. Thus, the old saw in law, "A Grand Jury can indict a ham sandwich," or not, should a multi-million dollar and politically connected legal team intervene.

As the investigation rotted from the head down, District Attorney Alex Hunter sought to restore confidence after the bungling of information from inside of his office and the police

Prostitution of Justice

to the press. The world shuddered and laughed at the circus in Boulder. The police leaked and undermined the D.A.'s office. The D.A.'s office responded in kind with its own leaks, fueling the rift between the two government agencies charged with pursuing justice and JonBenet's killer. The press, honest sharks smelling blood, used money and airtime as anti-personnel grenades on any player in the Little Miss JonBenet Murder Pageant. The public gasped at new revelations and rehashed old revelations. The Ramseys were rich. They were white. They had everything. Above all, they portrayed themselves as Christians. To their defense arrived Lou Smit, who cemented an alternate suspect to support his position.

As stated, when Hunter called for the grand jury to take over the case, Smit sued Hunter to testify before the grand jury. After Hunter hoodwinked the world, claiming pride in the work of the legally gagged jurors while refusing to sign the indictment, Smit sued Hunter a second time to regain possession of the PowerPoint presentation Hunter's office had paid him to prepare for the grand jury. Technically, that PowerPoint document belonged to his employer, the Boulder District Attorney's Office, a minor detail with the DA mucking around with his personal and professional loyalties divided.

Nevertheless, Smit's theory required that someone wander around the Ramsey house for hours before the family's return from the White's Christmas party. The intruder(s) wait for everyone to go to bed, then use a stun gun to overpower

Prostitution of Justice

JonBenet, feed her pineapple, sexually molest and murder her, clean her up, clean up after himself, herself, or themselves, and disappear as mysteriously as their meandering appearance(s).

Smit released that PowerPoint presentation, which was grand jury testimony given in secrecy, to the press. Newsweek got it on one anniversary of JonBenet's death.[19] NBC's Good Morning America,[20] the next. He claimed he worked "for free," taking no compensation from the Ramseys. Well, he got some legal strategy and assistance from somewhere to barge into grand jury proceedings and take his PowerPoint presentation. That kind of legal clout can cost more than most retired cops keep in a nest egg. Smit did not have to face a citation for contempt of court for making public his grand jury testimony, courtesy of the District Attorney's office.

Linda Hoffman-Pugh, however, the Ramseys' housekeeper, only won her right to air the contents of her testimony after a legal action brought by victim's rights attorney Darnay Hoffman, the same troublemaker who hired handwriting experts and filed affidavits, fingering Patsy.

The Ramseys and their attorneys continued to cry "Intruder" for over a decade until the arrival of a wing nut named John Mark Karr. Brothers David and Ellis Armstead, investigators who worked the case in the first critical years for the Ramseys, well-paid as they were, found nothing to substantiate an intruder theory. Nevertheless, when Carol McKinley at Fox News reported in 2002 that authorities had

Prostitution of Justice

found no evidence of an intruder, the Ramseys sued the reporter and the network. The Federal District Court in Denver, the Honorable Phil Figa, ultimately dismissed the lawsuit on January 7, 2005. The judge stated in the dismissal that the Ramseys would be better served by the court of public opinion than by civil actions.[21]

Many journalists willingly complied with spreading an Intruder Theory over outrage. Carol McKinley had worked for years as a reporter for KOA Radio in Denver and had developed long-term relationships with the Colorado Bureau of Investigation, DAs' offices, and innumerable other police and local sources. She used her sources in the Ramsey case to air stories that became a stepping-stone to the national stage on Fox News. Bright, attractive, and photogenic, McKinley helped give the Ramsey case legs. Although journalists like to claim they do not pay for information, they often did in the Ramsey case, paying for hotels and meals, plane fares, and airport limousine services. Some paid a copyright fee or an honorarium, though only a fraction of what the tabloids paid. Carol McKinley also paid sources.

Ellis Armstead, through his constant presence and relentless investigation, provided a huge source of frustration for Boulder police detectives trying to put their case together against John and Patsy. When police detectives arrived to interview a relevant witness, they often found that Armstead's office had already taken a statement, a statement that could favor the defense, as the witness had already been prepared and would be trapped if a second statement did not comport with the first statement taken by Armstead. This strategy gave the Ramseys several important advantages.

When a police investigator takes a statement, the information becomes discoverable to defense attorneys only after charges are filed. However, statements taken by the defense before charges occur don't get into the hands of the prosecution unless the information favors the defendant. The defense investigator getting a jump on the police has an opportunity to lead the witness to make the "right" kind of statement. In the Ramsey case, leaks from Hunter's office reached Haddon's law firm and thus provided Armstead with the knowledge about whom the police next planned to interview. By getting to the witness first, Armstead could not only learn what the witness had to say but also how that witness would recall events in any subsequent police interview.

Ellis Armstead himself acknowledged his professional, rather than moral, commitment to John and Patsy once he resigned. "It was not like I was naïve. It wouldn't have changed how I did anything. It really didn't matter to me whether they did it or didn't do it."[22] His investigation did not spring from Christian discipline or naivete. As a hardened professional, it made no difference who killed JnsonBenet Ramsey. He worked for the defense, and the defense paid him for his loyalty.

Prostitution of Justice

The public looks to their own conscience and their children and can understand why some people believe or disbelieve John and Patsy. Devout Christians may question respected members of the community who could have murdered their daughter or that nine-year-old Burke could have somehow been involved. Patsy raised her finger on national television to warn parents in Boulder, "Hold your babies close. There's a killer out there."[23] Her voice cracked while John methodically recounted how they were a "normal"[24] family: the normal family that dressed six-year-old JonBenet in glamour makeup, scantily clad as a Las Vegas showgirl. We must ignore these images in order to accept John and Patsy's concept of "normal." Yet, long before October 13, 1999, the day of the release of the grand jury results, Alex Hunter had decided he would not sign a true bill to indict the Ramseys for child abuse resulting in death nor charge the couple as each other's accessory.

The difference between probable cause for police officers and probable cause for the grand jury lies both in the way the evidence is obtained and in its presentation. In Colorado law, the police most commonly make an arrest and provide their evidence to the district attorney's office, and that office makes the charging decision. Few felony cases come to a Colorado District Court through grand jury indictment. The district attorney certainly does not need "proof beyond a reasonable doubt" to file charges. Judges routinely find probable cause based on the testimony of police officers. Hunter could not have doubted that the Boulder Police Department believed they had probable cause to file charges. He just didn't have any prospects for a plea bargain with the Ramseys, nor the guts or integrity to face Hal Haddon, his political benefactor, and his world-class defense team in court.

The grand jury assembled in Boulder in 1998. It received testimony from the police, the Ramseys' housekeeper, Linda Hoffman-Pugh, Burke Ramsey (who admitted to being awake), cops, and many others, including Lou Smit, the religious zealot and respected investigator. Smit had passionately committed himself to John and Patsy's innocence. He also demanded to testify before the Boulder District Court Grand Jury when he wasn't subpoenaed, thanks to significant legal assistance. He said his resignation from the investigation had nothing to do with the religion he shared with John and Patsy. He insisted that only an intruder could have murdered JonBenet. "I've arrested a lot of Christians," he said, defending himself against the reasonable assumption that his support of the Ramseys was driven by his shared religious beliefs.

Prostitution of Justice

Chapter Nine: Real NEWS Fake NEWS

As early as October 25, 1999, days after Alex Hunter declared no indictments in the murder of JonBenet, Smit's intruder theory gained respectability. After all, if the grand jury indicted no one, didn't it have to be an intruder? Thus, by refusing to sign the indictment of John and Patsy Ramsey and hiding their potential culpability from the public, Alex Hunter gave Lou Smit and his theory national respectability. Appearing on Good Morning America with Katie Couric, the network willingly replayed Smit's intruder theory for sweeps, running a five-day series during ratings week, and by doing so, cemented Smit's credibility and his theory.[25] Those photographs that The *Globe* had obtained in January 1997, the coroner's photos that were removed from newsstands, were used on the Good Morning America telecast. Those once forbidden photos hit the ratings buttons and still thrill ghouls with their publication on the internet.

The private investigator and lab technician who had supplied the gruesome images to the *Globe* paid a criminal price. But, damn, JonBenet sold newspapers!

Time Magazine ran Smit's intruder theory on October 25, 1999.[26] Time did not publish the gruesome autopsy photographs that Smit presented to the grand jury and used on Good Morning America. Smit also never faced a lawsuit from

Prostitution of Justice

John or Patsy Ramsey, nor would any media willing to milk the intruder theory.

The media, now selling Smit's version of the crime, cast Patsy as a victim, the innocent mother of overzealous police work. And, for Patsy, these revivals returned the former Miss West Virginia to the limelight. Smit need not have worried about being charged for his pornographic display of the dead child's body. Once again, long after her death, the invasion of JonBenet's privacy was welcomed so long as it aligned with saleable images, ratings, and advertising revenue.

Ramseys' tell-all book, *The Death of Innocence*, first published in 2000, provides a splendid inside examination of the parents' side of the story. Its publication was expertly marketed after the scales of justice had weighed enough ink on theories to raise doubts. The Ramseys followed tactics used by the O.J. Simpson defense team to paint the accuser, the Boulder police, as having a "rush to judgment"[27] from the outset of the investigation. Through that "rush," Boulder police overlooked evidence of harder-to-find suspects. As in Simpson's defense, which claimed that none of the "invisible" evidence of Colombian drug lords, police planting evidence, and laboratory conspirators was taken seriously, the Ramsey case suggests that all the evidence of an intruder was there but happened to be "invisible." Police unfairly ignored the invisible clues, the Ramseys maintain, in favor of visible evidence, like the ransom note or the fibers from Patsy's sweater under the tape covering the dead child's mouth. According to the Ramsey version of their daughter's death, the Boulder police never bothered to look beyond the Ramseys for suspects.

Nonsense! The protests of John and Patsy forced the Boulder police to invest hundreds, then thousands, of staff hours identifying, locating, and interviewing any conceivable witness and likely or unlikely suspect. In all, they considered 147 alternate suspects and cleared each and every one of them. They needed to do so not only because of their professional responsibility but also to avoid the Ramseys' accusation that the police failed to consider anyone but them as possible suspects.

Ellis Armstead, the private investigator for the Ramseys, and his staff did not work under intense public pressure to investigate every person on the list. Most of the people on their list were as improbably suspicious as Santa Claus. (And, as a matter of fact, Santa Claus, portrayed by local teacher Bill McReynolds, was on the suspect list.) Armstead and his investigators worked at the direction of the defense, beating the police to key witnesses and presenting their public effort to develop alternate suspects. The Ramseys never complained of their or their lawyers' "rush to judgment" in accusing friends and identifying an occasional poor and helpless man or woman as a suspect.

Hunter and his office would have the public believe that they found themselves at a loss to determine any cause, probable or improbable. Perhaps this had something to do with

Prostitution of Justice

the fact that Hal Haddon, mastermind of the Ramsey defense team, provided an umbrella of legal protection few but the Ramseys could buy. As for those who might produce probable cause and who could not be forced into silence, Ramsey's money bought political influence and opened courtroom doors for their prosecutions or lawsuits to silence them.

Volumes can and have been written about the flawed police work that morning of JonBenét's disappearance before her body's discovery. Police consideration for the Ramseys' "grief" let them escape the routine police procedure when a murdered child is found in the home of their parents. Instead, the police gave the ransom note back to the Ramseys.

Donald Vacca, a twenty-five-year veteran of the Denver Police Department, had retired from law enforcement and, at the time of JonBenét's death, augmented his pension as a handwriting expert. He worked from his home in Evergreen, Colorado. The Ramseys' criminal defense team hired Vacca, ostensibly to perform handwriting analysis on the ransom letter that Patsy had "found." He never published a written report. Mr. Vacca also signed a confidentiality and publishing agreement with John and Patsy, not through their lawyers,[28] that would ensure his silence.

In fact, some handwriting experts retained by the Ramseys in their criminal defense became involved in the publicity campaign early on before Newsweek had published the facsimile of the ransom note. Whoever the Ramsey expert was had taken several individual letters out of context and published a newspaper advertisement asking if anyone knew of someone whose handwriting showed these characteristics. "Do you know anyone who writes an 'M' like this?" the advertisement read.[29] If so, Team Ramsey wanted to talk and to turn all those fingers pointing at Patsy in another direction, any other direction. This produced some headlines but no results.

Hal Haddon, the genius of Ramsey's criminal defense team at Denver's Haddon, Morgan, and Foreman moved on to defend the fabulously wealthy NBA star Kobe Bryant, and his firm won a dismissal of rape charges. The press hounded Bryant's victim into silence. The rest of the phalanx of lawyers also moved on to new cases, less notorious cases, profitable cases that attract less scrutiny and less cynicism from the press. The press moved on. It broke camp the day Boulder District Attorney Alex Hunter announced that the grand jury investigating the death of JonBenet Ramsey would not file charges. The grand jury would not issue a report. It would not release the original ransom note. And, pursuant to a new Colorado law scandalously passed before the time of the grand jury's deliberations, the grand jurors would be silenced or face contempt of court and/or felony charges should they divulge any of the testimony or evidence they heard and examined. Additionally, no one could make any mention of the true bill signed for the indictment of the parents. It is impossible to imagine that such a law would be rushed through the Colorado legislature without some skullduggery by a party or parties who had an interest in silencing the grand jury's deliberations and findings.

With nothing left to report, the JonBenet Ramsey criminal inquiry, as well as the body of the child herself, would be abandoned. The citizens who made up the grand jury in Boulder and who had met for over a year would also be abandoned. The story of JonBenet's torture and murder did not die there. It lives now in American mythology.

Tomorrow, and the next day, and the day after that, another little girl will be murdered by her mother or father, brother, uncle, aunt, stepparent, or guardian, maybe for bedwetting or crying too long, maybe for sexual pleasure or revenge. Maybe a new boyfriend doesn't like small-voiced backtalk; maybe the child is murdered because she's inconvenient, or maybe by accident. Her adult caretakers will be taken into custody, questioned separately, and lacking a reputation as "credible millionaires," as Boulder Police Detective Commander John Eller described the Ramseys, they would be arrested and trying to raise a $1,000,000 bond.

Average citizens do not receive any evidence pointing toward other suspects. Average citizens do not have lawyers and consultants to create invisible evidence and make it stick. Average citizens face a tax-supported investigation and prosecution with an average lawyer and little money. The public defender assigned to the case will seek a plea bargain.

Prostitution of Justice

The local district attorney will ask for decades, or scores, or life, or a death sentence if strong enough evidence exists. Children are murdered by their parents all too often. Their stories die, but the JonBenet story rises like the Ghost of Christmas Past, her unbelievably brutal story cemented in American history as firmly as Charles Dickens's fiction in English literature.

The next little girl's name will not become a household word synonymous with mystery and lust, not if her parents are poor. The elements that keep JonBenet's story and name alive, unlike that of most child victims, are those of a sexualized child, fairy tale, and gothic titillation. The legal system will grind on, freeing the rich and the guilty less often than the rich and the innocent, but very reluctantly, the poor, regardless of guilt or innocence. The working class and the poor do not have the fees to support the lawyer's standard of living. The public defender's office has neither the staff nor the time to meet the crush of new cases arriving every morning and afternoon at the court docket. A public defender has no political clout.

The media will continue making crime specials starring Lizzie Borden, the Lindbergh kidnapping, Patty Hearst, O.J. Simpson, Princess Diana, Michael Jackson, and JonBenet Ramsey "news" or crime specials. The beauty princess's murder is not quite so gory as that of Lizzie Borden's hacked-up parents, though easily more glamorous than the Lindbergh kidnapping. Lacking a trial like those other "crimes of the century," hers must remain a mystery of sexual innuendo, taboo, and the prostitution of American criminal justice.

With Patsy Ramsey's death on June 24, 2006, twelve jurors will never hear the evidence against her in a courtroom. Instead, an expensive and manufactured reasonable doubt replaced the American courtroom with a 24/7 Odyssean siren of a crackpot intruder theory and an occasional crackpot who claimed to be an intruder. By delaying a decision, Alex Hunter gave rumor and gossip electronic wings, redirecting public outrage into speculation.

Never having enough confidence in his prosecutors and with a clear political interest in not filing charges, Hunter shirked his responsibility to charge and convened the grand jury. By then, the invisible evidence, talk show interviews, and Lou Smit's miracle "Intruder" intervention reduced common sense to irrelevancy. The new public relations standard for "guilt beyond a reasonable doubt," even "probable cause," lay upon a golden threshold only the rich, and the very rich at that, could cross.

On October 25, 2013, Boulder Judge J. Robert Lowenbach released grand jury transcripts from 1999 indicting John and Patsy Ramsey to the public. The foreman of the grand jury signed a true bill to indict each parent for child abuse resulting in death and conspiracy for assisting a person in the crime of first-degree murder. The story of the indictment lies somewhere within the millions of hits the phrase "JonBenet

Ramsey" receives on the internet. The unsigned indictment and the gagged jurors remain inexplicably unimportant.

Boulder District Attorney Alex Hunter, after announcing the grand jury "decision," claimed, politically, "We do not have sufficient evidence to warrant the filing of charges." That was a lie.

The ending of the Ramsey case now lies in folktales of American mythology, with no better ending than a savage killing and no justice for the child. In this "fairy tale" ending, did the jealous queen want to get rid of the Cinderella princess? Look how quickly the popular press went from accusing John to accusing Patsy. In fairy tales, the king is usually not guilty of killing his princess, although he will often abandon her for his son or second wife.

The decision on Hunter's part not to indict came in concert with the strategy of Haddon, Morgan, and Foreman to claim any "bad fact"—any fact—that pointed to the Ramseys' involvement in their daughter's death, as a non-fact, a falsehood, and confirmed a non-fact with the influence of the press' recycled tales of Lou Smit's "invisible" evidence like a stun gun. Hunter faced the "bad fact" of Professor Foster's sympathy note to Patsy and dodged it. If he publicly accepted the truth of the expert's analysis, he would have to face, on national television, a criminal defense team with courtroom skills his office could never match.

Prostitution of Justice

Hunter knew something way back in 1998. A member of his staff, Trip DeMuth, reviewed the search warrant. The search warrant requested potential child pornography, but it did not list writing samples to compare with the ransom note! Hunter complained to tabloid reporter Craig Lewis and other members of the press that his office needed a "break," a new revelation, to indict the Ramseys. The unfortunate fact is that District Attorney Hunter ignored all the breaks that came his way, except for immediately reporting them via a tabloid press leak to the Ramseys' defense attorneys. While this did not necessarily render the leaked evidence inadmissible in court, it provided the Ramseys' lawyers information that they could not have expected to receive prior to the filing of charges. The leaks armed the defense with the opportunity to undermine confidential work performed by police officials and to campaign to the press that no "fair" trial was possible because of the leaks. John and Patsy's public relations consultants and the press then spun real evidentiary facts out to the public with their own response, which was to exaggerate and trivialize, deny, and calumniate the source.

John and Patsy also sued, and Burke Ramsey later sued news sources, networks, or voices, accusing Burke of being a suspect. Witness the record: St. Martin's Press, Time Inc., The Fox News Channel, American Media, Inc., The Star, The *Globe*, Court TV, The New York Post, Windsor House

Publishing Group, and CBS News, for $1 billion, settled out of court for an undisclosed amount.

The Ramseys have also been sued for statements they made in their tell-all, The Death of Innocence. Robert Christian Wolff, a *Boulder Daily Camera* reporter, sued for $50 million, claiming John Ramsey defamed him in a March 24, 2000, NBC interview by Katie Couric. John Ramsey responded that he believed Wolff was a suspect early in the investigation and said, "This is it. This is the killer." Wolff's case was dismissed when the judge found an abundance of evidence supporting the intruder theory.[30]

Burke Ramsey was a month shy of being ten years old at the time of his sister's death. Under Colorado law, ten is the minimum age at which a child can be charged with murder. One may only speculate as to why the grand jury would not issue a report or ask only a child, Burke, one of the three persons in the Ramsey household on December 26, 1996, to testify, but not the parents. It is precisely the power of the grand jury to compel testimony by subpoena that enforces the search for truth.

When John Mark Karr, a pedophile who claimed he had killed JonBenet Ramsey, was arrested in Thailand in 2006, John Ramsey reminded everyone not to rush to judgment, as he and Patsy had suffered when the case was fresh, and Smit's intruder theory had gained traction. Karr, a 41-year-old American schoolteacher in Thailand, had fallen in love with JonBenet through her endless worldwide images. Finally, as an expression of his deep emotional attachment to the world of JonBenet Ramsey, or lust for fame, or the thrill of the lie, Karr confessed, falsely, to her murder.

Mary Keenan-Lacy, Boulder's pro-intruder theorist replacement for Alex Hunter as Boulder County District Attorney, quoted John's "poignant advice" not to rush to judgment in her news conference at the worldwide broadcast of Karr's arrest. Meanwhile, Boulder Detectives escorted Karr back from Thailand, first class, so Mr. Karr could sip champagne, feast on lobster, and hopefully reveal the intimate details of his confession, which he could not. He was cleared.

Mary Keenan-Lacy, who came to sympathize with John and Patsy, more than befriended the tragedy-torn couple but went on to clear the Ramseys of suspicion in 2008, to the amazement of prosecutors, as the killer(s) remained at large.

Belief in the Ramseys' innocence, at least in their friends' eyes, mattered as a test of faith. Yet, for those who believed in things visible to see, believing the Ramseys' story about their actions and recollections on the night their little girl was being tortured and killed ("We were asleep.") required a leap of faith at which Kierkegaard might blanch.

To bolster their claim of innocence, the Ramseys employed one of the most highly respected "profilers" in the United States, John Douglas. Novelist Thomas Harris, in The Silence of the Lambs, based his character on Mike Crawford, the FBI's head of its emerging staff of criminal profilers, on John Douglas. The movie The Silence of the Lambs made John Douglas famous. John Ramsey hired Douglas to disseminate a "profile" of a theoretical intruder. In his book, *The Cases that Haunt Us*, Douglas describes the killer as a relatively young white male with a grudge against Ramsey. The killer, as this theory goes, had been determined to take and defile Ramsey's most valuable thing in the world—JonBenet.[31]

Except for being a middle-aged female cancer survivor, John Douglas' intruder matches the profile of Patsy Ramsey in Dr. Andrew Hodges's first book, *A Mother Gone Bad*.[32] Dr. Hodges sees Patsy as jealous of the relationship between her husband and their precociously sexual daughter. Douglas, however, denies the possibility that Patsy wrote the ransom note. The famous profiler does admit that the ransom note is a key piece of evidence, likely written by the murderer before the murder. (That's Lou Smit's position.) Douglas admits that the $118,000 ransom figure indicates a person who wants to hurt John, yet he can't fathom the personality revealed in the note. Had one of the most renowned profilers in the world failed to notice the resemblance between his employer's wife's personality and the "intruder's?" Douglas will admit only to working for John, not Patsy, and John does not fit his profile except for being male. He states that he gave the Ramsey legal team the same explanation he gave any other client before accepting employment, including notice that while his services were for sale, his conclusions, good or bad, were not.[33]

Lou Smit could have influenced Douglas' analysis. Douglas states as much in *The Cases that Haunt Us,* when he came to rely on Smit's theory as a confirmation of his own independent analysis.[34] Lou Smit also led Douglas to include invisible evidence of a stun gun never found at the scene of the crime. Since both worked for the defense, it is fortunate that his unbiased conclusion drew inspiration from the creator of the intruder theory, if not tainted with filthy lucre.

Patsy does not fit the John Douglas profile. She does fit the profile of other profilers and professionals. When Dr. Hodges completed his research and published his second book, *Who Will Speak for JonBenet?* he found clues to the personality of the ransom note writer, enough for him to identify Patsy Ramsey, the mother of the dead child, as the writer.[35]

Bill Hagmaier of the FBI's Child Abduction and Serial Killer Unit assisted the Boulder police in the Ramsey investigation, as did others skilled in profiling. Hagmaier and his colleagues did not support Douglas' opinion that the Ramseys were not involved in their daughter's death. Instead, these experts agreed that the "kidnapping" was staged, and the crime scene pointed to the parents.

On June 1 and June 2, 1998, the Boulder police met with members of Hunter's office to present their case for charging

John and Patsy Ramsey. Hagmaier and his team attended. According to former Boulder Detective Steve Thomas, Hagmaier expressed his concerns that the parents may have been involved and that the district attorney, Alex Hunter, needed to act. His suggestion did not meet with Hunter's real concern, a political one.[36]

Bill Hagmaier, the FBI profiler initially on the case, did not state that Patsy Ramsey did not write the note. Recognizing the circus in Boulder that the Ramsey case had become an embarrassment to law enforcement, the FBI disentangled itself and returned to headquarters.

In the end, Hunter showed that he had no stomach for the office he had held for 28 years. For months after the Ramsey investigation, things began to change. He showed up less for work, and video store receipts indicated he watched a lot of movies and adult films.

Prostitution of Justice

Chapter Ten: We Did It

On the afternoon of October 13, 1999, hundreds of persons, members of the media and citizens, gathered outside the Boulder Courthouse to hear the announcement of the grand jury investigation into the murder of JonBenet. The brilliant autumn colors of Boulder brightened the atmosphere, and the air grew electric under the shadows of dozens of antennae mounted on the mobile television vans. A carload of teenage girls drove by on Canyon Boulevard and shouted out in unison, "We did it!" The air split into peals of laughter.

Inside the courthouse, Hunter called one of his favorite reporters, Craig Lewis of the *Globe*, to tell him there would be no charges. Craig Lewis walked Hunter from his office to the doors leading to the microphones and cameras. Lewis stopped inside the building, hidden from the eyes of the world. Hunter faced the cameras to claim the grand jury had done its work. He did not tell the truth as to their decision to charge John and Patsy Ramsey, which was ignored.

The media said a few polite goodbyes to those it had used. Released from their duties to report, their mop-up interviews and old stories waited in the files of newspaper morgues and live again in internet searches. The media camp in Boulder broke, the reporters scattered, and the media vans set out for the next scandal-ridden entertainment. What a pity!

Prostitution of Justice

Boulder is a journalist's dream assignment with upscale restaurants, well-placed sources, and the Flatirons to the west for extraordinary background shots. Best of all, Boulder had a district attorney's office as full of leaks as a colander. The story died, and the myth began.

The Boulder police had to accept Hunter's decision with more profound sadness than the media. Many outside the press who followed this case sat stunned. The claim that Hunter's district attorney's office didn't have "sufficient evidence to warrant the filing of charges against anyone who had been investigated"[37] was never true. Boulder police knew it. Hunter knew it, and so did any criminal defense lawyer.

By 2006, Boulder's District Attorney, Mary Keenan-Lacy, offered another low point in the Ramsey case with the faithless arrest of John Mark Karr. Hunter could not find probable cause to arrest anyone who was at the house Christmas night, 1996, armed with a grand jury indictment he refused to sign. Conversely, Lacy created the international hoax out of Karr's "confession." Instead of acting as Boulder's chief law enforcement officer, Lacy became an intruder-theory mouthpiece. She poisoned any hope for justice by claiming that her investigation of John and Patsy Ramsey had cleared them of their child's death.

The unsigned true bill for the indictment of John and Patsy Ramsey for Child Abuse Resulting in Death and as co-conspirators did not receive much sunlight.

Prostitution of Justice

It produces an internet search, but very few people know of it or have looked it up since its publication on October 25, 2013, fourteen years after the murder, after the circus had packed up and left Boulder, after Patsy died, after the truth finally crept out and was ignored, assigned to a footnote in the mythology. No Larry King interviews or furled talking heads are now aware that the intruder theory didn't carry water for the grand jurors, nor did it alter history.

No matter the examination of facts, a compilation of rumors, or strongly held opinions, a bald accusation that any of the family members murdered JonBenet can still result in a defamation lawsuit. Breakdowns in the criminal justice system do not prevent civil courts from enforcing "silence" upon outsiders or voyeurs who have no "proof beyond a reasonable doubt" or a substantiated confession. Courts and juries exist to determine guilt. Absent a judgment with its legal imprimatur, the published accusation of "murderer" naming anyone, family member or an identified mysterious intruder without the verdict of "guilt beyond a reasonable doubt" exposes the accuser to civil retribution. One may ponder, opine, or believe that John, Patsy, or Burke Ramsey committed murder based upon any compilation of facts, but the publication of such an opinion or belief denies due process to the accused. Broken or efficient, the American civil justice system is designed and works efficiently, to punish an unproven truth. Many

Prostitution of Justice

have accused JonBenet's family members of "hiding behind their lawyers." That is their right, and they have the financial wherewithal to enforce it.

The murder mystery nears its entry into a fourth decade. No one will be charged for causing JonBenet's death, nor her torture, nor her sexual molestation, much to the disappointment of the tens or hundreds of thousands or millions of followers of the case on the internet. The absence of charges and the failure of the criminal justice system are exactly the reasons that those minions of the mystery continue to examine every aspect of the case, find suspects for accusations, and dismiss claims against others. As of this writing, Reddit, the American social news website, has 86,000 followers of the JonBenet Ramsey case who continue to examine, analyze, condemn, praise, and debate every aspect of the case, from clues to suspects to lies.

John, Patsy, and Burke Ramsey may remain suspects, but they will never be found guilty of JonBenet's murder. That's the law.

Prostitution of Justice

Prostitution of Justice

Part Two
The JonBenet Ramsey Murder Pageant

Chautauqua Park - Boulder, Colorado

Prostitution of Justice

Chapter One: The Curse

When Fleet White stood up, he stood out. A tall man in any room, he stood with confidence, had an easy smile, and a broad-shouldered, rangy physical presence. He had a small cleft in his chin, thin lips, and light brown hair, now gray. He usually dressed casually like most of the well-to-do in Boulder and carried the airiness of a fortunate life like a gentleman. A few crow's feet tracked from his wizened blue eyes and lightly freckled face. Blessed, he grew up in a wealthy family invested in minerals and oil, and he married the love of his life, Priscilla, four years younger than him, whom he met in college.

Like Fleet, Priscilla White had blue eyes but with high-arching eyebrows under bangs, a long oval face, and high cheekbones. Her lips usually held a smile, mischievous and innocent, with bemusement underlying the pistol she was. A smart, lean woman with reddish-brown hair flowing over her shoulders, people found her happy and full of laughter, with her strength in God and her heart filled with family. Fleet and Priscilla grew up in California, with coastlines and beaches, where the Pacific Ocean offers sailing next to a land of earthquakes. The San Andreas Fault had threatened their world too many times. Born into comfort and privilege, raised in

Prostitution of Justice

family values, they sought a new, safer home to raise their two young children. They found Boulder, a city like no other Colorado zip code. Just as every urban center develops its own personality, this college town amalgamated its history of academics since 1876 with farming and ranching into an erstwhile highly educated community with its attention on ecology, soil conservation, and technology.

Its proximity, 36 miles south of Rocky Mountain National Park, also made it a tourist respite on the way north from Denver. Boulder had also become an upscale drug and party Mecca since the 1960s. The scenic location debuted comedian Robin Williams' career in the television sitcom Mork and Mindy. Before JonBenét's murder exposed its dysfunctional criminal justice system, Boulder's residents complained mostly about fraternity pranks and loud parties, demurring with an amused smile to Boulder's description as "twenty square miles surrounded by reality."

Before making their home investment in the pricey Boulder real estate market, Fleet and Priscilla White rented a comfortable home on the Hill, two doors down from John and Patsy Ramsey. Burke and JonBenet were close in age to their children, Fleet, Jr., and Daphne. The steeply rising foothill neighborhood on the Hill west of the University of Colorado campus housed an eccentric mix of college students, frat houses, professors, professionals, high-tech entrepreneurs, middle-aged hippies, highly educated men and women with

Prostitution of Justice

children, and group homes for schizophrenics among the other homeless, drug-addicted, and alcoholic who often tracked up Baseline Rd. from the exit off U.S. Highway 36 past the fine homes of the well-to-do to Chautauqua Park.

Relationship with like-minded neighbors and church members, many of whom came from Patsy Ramsey's expansive group of social contacts. Before her move from Atlanta, Patsy had organized fund-raising charitable groups, one of which was called Socia-Tea. Once ensconced in Boulder, Patsy continued her social groups and formed the Moms Gone Bad Softball Team, sponsored by John's company. The recruits came from church members, neighbors, and friends: mothers who could arrange for childcare while they went to afternoon practices, leave dinner to restaurants, crockpots, or household help to play in an oasis from responsibility. Their spouses and children specifically were not invited to practices, only to games.

With her lanky and athletic body, Priscilla could catch, run, and bat, doing it all with ease and balance. At an annual Ramsey Christmas Party before the tragedy, Priscilla appeared at the kitchen doorway. As guests turned to look at her, she leaped into the kitchen, landing on her knees to slide across the black and white checkered floor with a glass of wine in hand. She never spilled a drop. The guests cracked up and applauded. She carried that knack for goofing around with friends at parties to softball practices, cutting up with a few dance steps and lines from a popular song, or rolling an audience with a self-deprecating humor. She gave everyone permission to have fun, to laugh, to take chances, to enjoy life. Her mischievous side notwithstanding, Priscilla wrapped her arms around her husband and children with all her charity under Fleet's protection.

The White family eventually bought a home a mile up Baseline Rd. from the Ramseys, a home with windows, sunlight, and shade trees on a big lot just south of Chautauqua Park. As a leader in his community, Fleet attended parent-teacher conferences and school board meetings and made sure he and his children received that world-class, diverse education the high Boulder property taxes should provide. He carried the voices of fellow church members as well as neighbors with him to meetings: the Ramseys, the Phillipses, the Steins, the Walkers, Helen Rogers and her sons, all friends, all parents with children. Daphne White called JonBenet her best friend, and her parents were equally close to the Ramseys.

JonBenet also had a friend in Boulder who had been born in Georgia, Lindsey Phillips, who was only a month younger than Burke. Patsy Ramsey and Judith Phillips, Lindsey's mother, were friends in Atlanta and had shared their pregnancy experiences with each other in "Hotlanta." Daphne White and her older brother, Fleet Jr., played with the many friends from the Ramsey circle, including Lindsey. Though only a month younger than Burke, Lindsey preferred the company of JonBenet. "Everyone knew Burke was smart, but

Prostitution of Justice

all he wanted to do was play video games," Lindsey remembered. JonBenet's brother did have one close friend, Doug Stein, who joined Burke in video gaming. One sentence described Doug Stein: "He was well-dressed, proper, and condescending," according to Lindsey Phillips.

Just for fun, JonBenet and her playmates would sneak downstairs to gather near the basement room as Burke and Doug stared oblivious to anything other than the screen, buttoning furiously, crushing each other with animatronic clubs, conquering shield maidens. For laughs and real fury, JonBenet would unplug the television, mid-game, mid-button, and then everyone screamed in high-tempo laughter as the two gamers chased JonBenet's gang of friends from their basement lair.

JonBenet's friends accepted Burke's isolation as his role in the family sank from first son to ignored older sibling. Patsy, Nedra, and Aunt Pam had JonBenet to dress, coif, and polish in a clucking fuss of beauty pageantry. Patsy loved photographs of her family, but the walls of the house mostly displayed Burke's sister in gowns and tiaras wearing ribbons. Of course, John Ramsey loved his son, as did Patsy, but John headed up a growing tech company valued in the hundreds of millions that would eventually become a possession of aeronautics giant Lockheed Martin. He had to concentrate on the demands of the office while Patsy & Company crushed the credit cards, leaving Burke to his video games while working the pageant circuit with this jewel, this living treasure, JonBenet, whom they intended to win the crown as Miss America.

Once the little beauty died, John and Patsy built a Hadrian's Wall of protection around Burke. Bodyguards escorted him to school, attended his classes, and shielded him from any associations outside his parents' approval. Burke's delicacy, pain, and silence became a fortress of protection and counseling. He did not speak publicly about the death of his sister for 20 years until an interview on the Dr. Phil television show on December 12, 2016.

After JonBenet's murder and during the funeral back in Georgia, the CNN interview staged in Atlanta offended Fleet and Priscilla. Cheap theatrics! Tabloid! Then, the blowup, a police call, and another target as John Ramsey named Fleet White as a prime suspect. The press smelled out a blood rage, and their teeth came out in diverse headlines of Fleet White's guilt or innocence, depending on how the tabloids wished to eat the little fish netted in the banquet of headline-churning waves.

Lead Boulder P.D. investigator Steve Thomas, with partner Tom Trujillo, flew to Atlanta. They witnessed the drama from box seats provided by the professional courtesy of the Atlanta Police Department. Thomas arrived as the first detective after Commander John Eller at the Ramseys' on the morning of December 26, 1996. He had joined Boulder P.D. 13 years earlier, and he had risen to become the lead investigator for the biggest murder in Boulder's history. He had never investigated a murder because murders were exceedingly rare in Boulder, Colorado.

Thomas had wide lips that could hold a secret. His smile didn't show his teeth, appearing more whimsical, only happily amused. Thomas projected confidence, was well-groomed, and had the handsome face of a resolute servant of justice. He became a Christian knight willing to draw his sword against the tabloid dragon pouring their lurid flames upon justice. He raised his voice against the humiliation and the muckraking tabloids he saw in grocery store check-out lines. As he did his job, forming an unshakable opinion that Patsy Ramsey murdered JonBenet over a bedwetting incident, he promised some of those banished from the Ramseys' circle that he would host a picnic at Chautauqua Park once he solved the case.

As Thomas and Trujillo took back-row seats attending JonBenet's funeral, they took notes and picked up on the background chatter. They learned from Atlanta police officers about a dust-up between the Ramseys and the Whites. Fleet White questioned John Ramsey's cry of innocence in the CNN interview, which came across, with Patsy's tears and dramatic warnings to "keep your babies close to you,"[38] as way too tabloid. The Ramseys had also named many suspects, friends, and business associates. Patsy had tossed her housekeeper, Linda Hoffman Pugh, to the wolves for tattling about JonBenet's bedwetting and fecal soiling. The many accusations crushed friendships as they darkened reputations and left the

Prostitution of Justice

accused in the arena of the tabloids, as suspects in time-crushing demands, along with personalized anxiety when Boulder P.D.'s detectives showed up with questions. Chief Tom Kolby and Alex Hunter dealt with the press. The Ramseys remained silent on the advice of counsel while their defense team sent out its investigators to beat the brush. Ramsey public relations experts outed "suspects" in press leaks like trophies for the hungry press.

It was while Detectives Thomas and Trujillo attended JonBenet's funeral in Atlanta that John Ramsey's and Fleet White's friendship ruptured. The local police investigated a 911 call involving the Whites and their Atlanta host, Jeff Ramsey. The dust-up became public enough to delight the press. Underneath the headlines, Thomas identified the alienation of the closest source from within the Ramsey circle: one who may speak with investigators, who distrusted and dismissed lawyers, and one whose Christian faith and belief in American justice did not settle easily onto the scales of Alex Hunter's justice. Like Brutus on Caesar, once Fleet White became alienated from the bereaved father of JonBenet, he questioned if his former close friend could have been complicit in the child's murder.

Unlike Fleet White, Steve Thomas did not grow up in a wealthy family, living a charmed life. He grew up in tragedy; his mother having died by suicide. No one experiences such a tragedy without a soul-shaking loss. Through that pain, through

Prostitution of Justice

the values of his family and his church, Steve Thomas grew up a devout Christian like Fleet and Priscilla White and Lou Smit.

Thomas and White are mixed-like characters from a Hollywood Western: one man wears a badge, and the other, a key witness, stands accused of a crime. Both want to catch the child-murdering monster in a town without pity. Thomas breathes the putrid miasma of poisoned evidence and watches money squeezing pus from the blind eyes of justice, choking in truth he has become certain of. Fleet White had once searched the basement of the Ramsey's mansion but did not find JonBenét's body. Decades later, neurotic bloggers still postulate that maybe he did find the body. Maybe he had committed the murder? The same could have been said of Officer Rick French when he failed to discover the child's body. French appeared merely incompetent, not homicidal.

John Ramsey would not let friendship interfere with his and Patsy's claim of innocence in their search for a culprit's involvement in JonBenet's murder. When Ramsey named Fleet White as a suspect, the accusation shadowed him, Priscilla, and their children through the unforgiving power of the press and its irresponsible bastard children: social media and the internet. Set adrift between the media sirens and the shoals of reality, White stood accused, exploited, and vilified as gutter snipes poured garbage theories over his reputation to blot his name. He remains international bait in the oceans of internet sharks.

Prostitution of Justice

An accounting of Fleet White and his family doesn't sum up into dull figures in green-skinned accountant's books, nor can the internet blasphemy and speculation account for his good character. Nevertheless, because of his prior friendship with John Ramsey and their well-publicized rupture, the press cast Fleet White into a scandalous mold to fill with speculation. Fleet White also stonewalled reporters. He stood with his shoulders back, his chin up, and in a John Wayne silence. The press gadflies did not like this quality. From the beginning, he would not speak to anyone outside of the police. Through the grand jury proceeding, he smelled out tabloids and found that their stench extended to all media—electronic, print, internet, or freelance writers—labeling all of them "Tabloid!"

Those who were less well off, those working stiffs like Steve Thomas, who needed to pay rent, became the bait, or in Thomas's case, trophies for big media to hunt. A good tabloid editor could select the tastiest, most prurient snacks for the feast. With cash and a little creative writing, reporters and editors hooked their stories and offered, with a little cash, a gleaming moment of fame. For the schools of little fish of no interest to the media, looking out their bedroom windows into the night sky, electrically connected and hungry to be a part of the international mystery, they could tap their keyboards and claim revelations that would solve the crime. The answers had to be there!

Prostitution of Justice

From newscasts and interviews, old photographs and tabloid pages grew a social media gourmet to chase, taste, and solve the JonBenet Ramsey Murder Investigation. No matter how cock-eyed the facts, the timelines, or distances, the new "Cybersleuths" could find self-satisfying "truths" that would harvest attention in chat rooms or websites that sprang up to meet the demand. All over the world, keyboards connected and brought international democracy to public investigation with mob rule of the information. Factions argued over the banquet of contradicting facts or posted volatile interpretations. Their opinions stood removed from censorship, and they were free to express any opinion, crazy, self-righteous, and sometimes, but rarely, correct. One garrulous opinion gained favor: Alex Hunter was in cahoots with the Ramsey legal team to send the investigation to the grand jury and stall it long enough to kill it.

The good and evil claims dividing the public became faces in the news. Sad, flesh sagging at his jowls, eyes beady behind his glasses, Alex Hunter represented "Justice" with his gambit, "We know who you are." Certainly, he would file charges soon. But then, months passed. Headlines blared: "No Charges in Beauty Princess' Murder."

Ruined cops began their own exit parade: Boulder P.D. Chief Tom Kolby had gone to Texas, and Lt. Jim Eller had gone to Florida. Linda Arndt resigned in 1999 and sued Chief Tom Kolby and the City of Boulder for scapegoating her in the flawed investigation. Larry Mason, her supervisor, also filed an

Prostitution of Justice

action against Boulder in Federal District Court for damaging his reputation. Boulder City Manager Tom Haney resigned and sued Boulder, trying to escape the curse of the Ramsey investigation. Many victims of the crime were crushed except Boulder P.D. Detective Steve Thomas. Although he resigned as he had investigated the case, he prospected for a better future outside of police work. In time, he profited by leaking the entire bizarre story of politics and the prostitution of JonBenet's murder from inside the Boulder P.D. and D.A.'s office to *Vanity Fair*.

Chapter Two: Crimes and Punishments

Soon after the *Globe* rushed Editor Joe Mullins from its Florida headquarters to Boulder, he had captured both the voyeur's market with the JonBenet autopsy photographs and the wrath of the tabloid-trouncing Ramseys, their defense team, friends, and local supporters. Craig Lewis, another tabloid editor, had similarly captured headlines in Los Angeles while covering the O.J. Simpson case for the *National Enquirer*. Lewis managed to buy Nicole Brown Simpson's diary. No one ever got the crime scene or autopsy photographs of Nicole Brown Simpson and Ron Goldman, though everyone glued to the media drooled to see them. They must have been ghastly, perhaps comparable to Jack the Ripper's product, with fury and blood everywhere. But the tabloids, try as they would, couldn't find anyone who would sell copies. The L.A.P.D. made sure reporters would not publish the coroner's film.

In contrast, Boulder, a small city with little experience in solving murders, had no concept of a tabloid's gangbang[39] approach to news. The autopsy photographs were taken from Dr. John Meyer's lab and sent to a local commercial developer, as they always had. The need for security did not occur to the coroner's office or the police. Boulder P.D. took the autopsy film to Photo Craft Laboratories, a local developer. Private investigator and former Boulder County Sheriff's Deputy Brett

Prostitution of Justice

Sawyer knew how the system worked and where to find the film. He also knew Larry Smith, a technician of nine years at the film lab. The banquet of tabloid photographs depicting violence and depravity committed on a six-year-old child came cheap. Sawyer paid Larry Smith all of $200 for over 100 images.

Sawyer had only worked for a short time as a deputy. He thought he could do better, and he did. He had a wife, a child, and, once he resigned from the sheriff's office, a successful private investigations business in Boulder. In sixteen years of investigation, Sawyer built up a dependable stable of New England insurance companies as clients. He earned twice as much as a cop. He handled disability and fraud investigations so successfully that his cases rarely went to litigation. To him, as with so many other private eyes in nearby Denver, the Ramsey case came as a windfall. With journalists from throughout the world scrambling for a scoop and tabloids spreading cash like manure on gardens for anything on the American beauty princess' death, the investigations business boomed.

Sawyer was married, and his six-year-old son attended the same elementary school as Burke and JonBenet Ramsey. Burke was his son's reading coach. The private investigator had majored in molecular biology and cultural anthropology at the University of Colorado before beginning his career in law enforcement and then private investigations. He had enjoyed learning the ropes of law enforcement but loved private investigations. All that changed after his meeting with Joe Mullins of the *Globe*.

With the sincerity of a serial killer courting his next victim, Mullins promised Sawyer that the *Globe* would not publish the autopsy photographs. The magazine just needed them for its own investigation and to inform the public. Preying on the former cop's desire to bring justice to JonBenet, the tabloid reporter explained that his publication had hired a world-famous forensic pathologist, Dr. Cyril Wecht, as a consultant to help solve the murder. Mullins retained Sawyer for $500 to locate the autopsy photographs and offered him a $5,000 bonus if he obtained them.

According to Sawyer, when he first looked at the photographs, "I saw immediately that this was a sex crime and not a kidnapping."[40] Perhaps the coroner, Dr. John E. Meyer, realized the same, but when he saw several photographs he had taken of JonBenet's corpse in the *Globe*, he saw red and called the cops. He had not released the photographs to anyone, nor had he given permission for their release. Like so many other citizens and professionals caught up in the most famous murder in Boulder's history, Dr. Meyer's reputation was at stake.

Larry Smith, the lab technician who sold the autopsy photographs to Sawyer, did not view them as did the Ramseys' public relations specialists, who had begun to shape a public outrage against the tabloids and to sell John and Patsy as victims. Smith thought he could help Sawyer solve the murder. He saw the incriminating weirdness and brutality at the crime scene in the prints. He thought, as did many reporters on the case, that the public, inflamed by the nature of the photographs, would press for a more rigorous investigation than that which had been carried out thus far.

The media hounded Boulder locals, friends, neighbors, and associates, as television, radio, and newspapers published their private stories throughout the community and beyond to the rest of the world when they intersected with the JonBenet Ramsey case. Ramsey claims that all communications with the press came from people beneath the dignity and character of Boulder's intelligent and culturally sophisticated population, which caused no end to derision and, sometimes, criminal charges. In fact, Boulder P.D. and the D.A.'s Office worked hand in hand to charge and jail those who came too close to the line between assisting a reporter and breaking the law.

The Ramseys could take satisfaction in a well-deserved public fury against the tabloids. The defense vilified the police for its lack of security. D.A. Alex Hunter threatened charges for leaking the photos and soon carried through with that intention. The Boulder police put muscle and manpower into investigating the leaked information that plagued the investigation, hoping to assuage earlier police blunders.

The purloined autopsy photographs further put into question the integrity of an already battered Boulder P.D.

Prostitution of Justice

Ramsey's lawyers could make a case that Boulder P.D. lacked professionalism and lodged an accusation of bad faith for letting the leak occur, adding fodder to the claim of a rush to judgment. The defense team also had a new hook to bait as it could coax public sympathy for the publication of the grotesque pictures for filthy lucre. This also added to a real claim that the Ramseys' right to privacy had been violated by the muckraking tabloids, as the world would see the savagery, the torture, and the debasement of little JonBenet Ramsey.

Most grocery and convenience stores in Boulder removed that week's *Globe* from their racks. In no way did this symbolic act protect Boulder, or its self-image, from knowledge of the little girl's last moments. Public momentum for charges against the Ramseys stalled as a perception of gross incompetence lodged against Boulder P.D. and Alex Hunter's D.A.'s office. The fickle nature of public opinion swung between demands for retribution against the Ramseys to increased pressure to either find the probable cause to charge the parents or find the elusive kidnapper who had turned into a sadistic murderer.

Patsy Ramsey melted her makeup with tears over the sensational use of the autopsy photographs. Few would blame her for that. Still, her frustration and lust for publicity could hardly be satiated. With the death of Princess Diana on August 31, 1997, she publicly identified with Princess Diana in the way the press had stalked Patsy as it had the Princess. She

Prostitution of Justice

emotionally connected her tragedy with that of international attention now focused on the death affecting the British monarchy. When CNN's Larry King brought Tony Frost, the editor of the tabloid The *Globe*, onto his talk show to discuss the deaths of Princess Diana and Dodi Fayed in an automobile accident during a high-speed pursuit by a gang of Paparazzi, Patsy Ramsey was watching the show. She grew incensed by Frost's denial of his interest in publishing gruesome photographs of the car wreck when he had used her daughter's autopsy photos. She reported her response of calling into the Larry King Show[41] to make this point as reported in her book, The Death of Innocence.

Patsy's recollection of those moments live on nationwide TV sounds almost dreamlike and quite angry. She expresses her need to begin by denigrating King for bringing a guest on air whom she considered utterly despicable. She and John would later appear on Larry King's program along with Boulder Detective Steve Thomas, who would accuse Patsy of the murder over a rage for a bedwetting incident. Patsy never thought of John or herself as despicable. Tony Frost, the *Globe* editor, was despicable. So was Steve Thomas. That's why they sued Thomas[42] for his accusation. Whatever Patsy wanted to know by calling in live to the Larry King Show, she certainly knew she'd bask in the spotlight and the headlines the following day.

Prostitution of Justice

Trusting the promise of anonymity for his work in producing the autopsy photographs and, perhaps, assistance in solving the murder, Brett Sawyer took private solace in having helped solve the crime. He selected seven out of more than 100 photographs that he believed would offer the greatest forensic value. When the *Globe* published the photographs days later, all hell broke loose. It didn't take a first-class "mind hunter" like the Ramseys' John Douglas to figure out that someone at Photo Craft must have delivered the photographs to Joe Mullins. The Boulder Police swooped down on Lawrence Smith, the Photo Craft employee who had processed the film, rather than on Sawyer. Smith denied it. The police pressured him to confess and administered a polygraph. Smith didn't crack when the machine confirmed to the police his role in copying and selling the photographs. Boulder P.D. could not force Smith to confess, and he refused to snitch on Sawyer.

On the day the *Globe* hit the newsstands, Sawyer had gone skiing. When he returned home, he found his voicemail full of calls from Joe Mullins.[43] The *Globe* reporter claimed he had no idea those bad-boy editors of his would use autopsy photographs the way they had. Sawyer realized he'd been had.

As a private investigator whose work frequently needed photographic evidence, Sawyer had worked with Larry Smith for nine years. The film technician knew that the private investigator had solved fraud cases, and he felt a sense of civic pride in developing the film and making the prints. Smith did

Prostitution of Justice

not know that his trusted friend would sell those gruesome photographs to the *Globe*. Neither Smith nor Sawyer knew that Joe Mullin had every intention of publishing the autopsy photographs in a nationally distributed tabloid rag. Neither could he know that the *Globe* would increase circulation by over a million, making more money than Sawyer or Smith could imagine for the paltry cost of acquiring the autopsy photographs. But they should have. The two luckless stooges of the media didn't know that their parts in trying to solve the murder would soon take their lives apart and that their demise would also appear on the front page of newsstands and on radio and television broadcasts worldwide. Smith knew only what he needed to know: Brett Sawyer, a private investigator he trusted, needed the photographs to solve the JonBenet Ramsey murder. Sawyer also knew what he needed: he looked forward to a $5000 bonus for producing the photos.

While the case had stalled at Hunter's office, Smith received $200 and believed he now had a hand in solving the murder. He never dreamed he had committed the felony. He would be charged with theft of more than $400. The film, the processing, and even the $200 Brett Sawyer paid him didn't amount to $400. Did the police value the profit from the "theft" by what those photographs were truly worth? Larry Smith had sold those photographs to Sawyer out of moral responsibility to JonBenet Ramsey, a civilized society, and had too little greed.

Prostitution of Justice

The parents and the traditional press took the position that the autopsy photographs had been "stolen." Sawyer had purchased copies while the negatives remained at Photo Craft. Did the cops have a proprietary right to copies of the photographs? Did the coroner? Would the rights of authorities to the photographs outweigh the First Amendment right of the press to obtain them and to publish them?

Boulder prosecutor Peter Hofstrom met Sawyer and his lawyer, Peter Shields. The prosecutor appeared cordial and apologetic. This whole Ramsey case had troubled him. Yes, the media had blown the issue out of proportion, but now both the coroner, Dr. Meyer, and the D.A. had to make an "example" of this case. The lawyers for the Ramseys had also expressed their outrage. They had a responsibility to their clients, and this release of evidence could poison the jury pool, which would likely play to a legal advantage. Still, they officiously demanded a lid on all these press leaks. The case had become a huge embarrassment to Boulder P.D., and they wanted to close the faucet on the leaks.

Assistant Boulder D.A., Pete Hofstrom, had read the *Globe*. He knew which tabloid editor dropped into Boulder, taking the lead and using the money for the autopsy photographs, but Joe Mullins had put just enough distance between himself and any criminal act to escape prosecution. He had merely hired an investigator. The press has not only a right, as a matter of the freedom of the press and free speech, to look

Prostitution of Justice

for information and ask questions but a responsibility to do so. Neither Mullins nor any other reporter had made a direct attempt to purchase the photographs from Photo Craft, Smith, or a police officer. Mullins didn't know whom to ask for the photographs outside of the coroner. Brett Sawyer did.

By mid-January 1997, the cops and the prosecutors had come to distrust each other, to belittle each other, and to snitch on each other. The defense strategy to exploit their considerable skill and reputation, coupled with political power and personal knowledge of Hunter's flexible character, worked as the problems at the top rolled downhill onto the police. Within the government, the Boulder police, and Hunter's office, no one could agree on where, when, why, or how this murder investigation should continue. They did agree that anyone who horned in on their contaminated and compromised investigation must pay for it.

Larry Smith, when he failed the lie detector test, had his chance to come clean. Stonewalling may pay off for big shots, but this working-class lab technician faced two felonies: theft of property over $400.00 and tampering with evidence, and two misdemeanors, obstructing government operations, and false reporting. As such, Photo Craft fired Smith. He had worked there for over nine years. He says he flushed the $200 cash down the toilet when he got caught and believed that his friend, Bret Sawyer, had betrayed him. He admitted his great mistakes and that he had ruined the rest of his life."[44]

Prostitution of Justice

Smith's mistake, once identified by the police, sent Brett Sawyer's life into a nosedive. All his insurance company clients terminated his services within twenty-four hours of the news breaking. Within the same twenty-four hours, the Boulder native became "the flavor of the day" for talk shows, networks, and wire services who smelled blood in the water. The BBC wanted Sawyer for interviews, but lawyers didn't want their clients' names sharing in his notoriety. He had to hide inside his mother's home with his wife and children in a nearby town for three days while satellite trucks circled his Boulder home.

The videos of JonBenet sexually sashaying in a skimpy cowgirl outfit raised the blood pressure of every pedophile in the world. The autopsy photographs titillated and horrified in a different way; they were exceptionally disturbing, the kind found by a medical examiner in Los Angeles, Paris, or Bangkok, not a Colorado mountain town. The world's hunger for the autopsy photographs and the public fascination with the display of the live child's body in the pageant videos stimulated each other. Had the Ramseys groomed an international sex object, dead or alive?

With the autopsy photographs, the press, the internet sleuths, and the rest of the world received raw meat for the story: flesh squeezed to death with a garrote, a broken paintbrush to probe a tiny vagina, and loosely tied ligatures at the little girl's wrists. The forbidden autopsy photographs offered a transposed pageantry, a staged kidnapping, and a dead child hidden in a basement house of horrors. The internet, still in its early stages, propelled the story into a furious, curious worldwide community that wanted answers and a willing group of amateur investigators willing to find or make up those answers.

Brett Sawyer sold his home in Boulder. He moved to a nearby community with lower mortgage payments. The family gave up dinners out. He worked for $8 to $10 per hour, still trying to revitalize his private investigations business. He and his wife cashed out their retirement, their savings, and their home equity. He answered death threats over the phone and found notes dropped on his table in local Boulder coffee shops with salutations such as "Dear Scumbag."[45]

Sawyer had grown up in Boulder: school, career, home, family. After the story broke, he feared for the safety of his son. He had uncovered, in his capacity as an investigator, smoking-gun evidence that whoever had killed JonBenet had not gone there for a kidnapping but did commit a sex crime. Sawyer had been paid to find evidence, like every other cop, investigator, or prosecutor, but his money came with a curse; it came from the tabloids.

Lawrnce Schiller, a renowned writer, wrote *Perfect Murder, Perfect Town*. He entered the JonBenet media meat market fresh from work on the O.J. Simpson case and the "Trial of the Century." During Schiller's months in Boulder, he became one of the most sure-footed purchasers of information,

Prostitution of Justice

enough for him to have produced the most thoroughly researched, read, and influential volume on the JonBenet Ramsey murder with coauthor Charlie Brennan. Craig Lewis and Schiller had known each other since O.J., and the author described Lewis' description as a "gang bang," a term of art for when the "tabs" dump dozens of editors, writers, photographers, and thousands in cash in every pocket to lock down the sources and stories by sundown.[46]

Lawrence Schiller liked Lewis enough to write the editor into his intruder mystery, even letting Lewis play himself in the made-for-TV movie based on his book *Perfect Murder, Perfect Town*. Lewis assisted, soon replacing Joe Mullins after the autopsy photos ran. Lewis had never met Brett Sawyer before parachuting into a delicate situation and exploiting the local hostility. He dug into the story with all fours like a charging bull, endangering the secrecy of any information, public or private, within the JonBenet Rubik's Cube.

Mentioning author Lawrence Schiller to Sawyer draws a "God damn him!"[47] He had given the "true crime" writer a long interview. What the private investigator thought Schiller would report as a careful review of the facts of his involvement became a "cartoon-like fiction." Schiller characterized Sawyer as a self-serving vulture, more concerned about the future of his concealed weapon permit than the grief and trouble he had caused and was in. The private investigator and a former cop held a rare, concealed weapon permit in Boulder, and therefore Colorado, and in

Prostitution of Justice

his line of work, he needed one. His permit was revoked.

"That wasn't what happened at all," Sawyer said. The difference between Schiller's published account and Sawyer's recollection of trying to solve a crime reduced Sawyer's search for justice into a self-mutilating journey. Sawyer's former good character and skill as a fraud investigator reveal his personal motive for discovering evidence of JonBenet's treatment at the hands of her murderer(s). Schiller wrote mostly about Sawyer's police contacts and his purchase of autopsy photographs. He didn't spend ink or time on Sawyer's observation that the autopsy photographs documented a sex crime, not a kidnapping, to the former cop and top-drawer private investigator.

What motive would the tabloids or any of their sources have for framing the Ramseys? A "small foreign faction" isn't the kind of story tabloid editors salivate over. "Six-Year-Old Glamour Girl Tortured and Murdered" sells! JonBenet sold! She still sells. Readers want facts—facts found, facts bought, facts sold in the tabloids—about this peculiarly fascinating murder that became no longer tabloid but mythological. The Ramseys asked the public to help them find the killer. How could anyone help if denied knowledge of the evidence, circumstances, and staging of the crime? The ransom note contained enormous details, gory in description but less distasteful than images of the mangled child.

Prostitution of Justice

Sawyer was hard to track down and harder to strike up a conversation with about his JonBenet Ramsey murder investigation. Whatever he saw in those 113 autopsy photographs, he will never talk about. He was neutralized as a witness with the smear of "tabloid" and ignored as an expert in crime and fraud. Sawyer finally found work in the computer industry.

Both Sawyer and Smith had signed on to help solve the mystery of a child's death. Instead, they entered the Big Top, center ring, of the Ramsey Murder Pageant. Sawyer learned hard lessons about blind justice. He learned that the criminal justice system bends to preserve the rich, the powerful, and the administration of the right kind of law.

Another victim of the JonBenet Ramsey investigation, Detective Steve Thomas, lead investigator, resigned from the Boulder P.D. in disgust when Alex Hunter made the political decision not to charge John and/or Patsy Ramsey, instead tossing that bomb to the grand jury. A month later, Intruder Theorist Lou Smit resigned in September 1998, only after the August 12, 1998, empanelment of a grand jury.

Steve Thomas had worn a white hat throughout his time on the case. He had promised select witnesses like Fleet and Priscilla White, Judith Phillips, and others who did not accept Ramsey's innocence that once he concluded his investigation and the Ramseys were charged, they would gather at Chautauqua Park for a picnic. Thomas and his investigators,

Prostitution of Justice

Ron Gossage and Tom Trujillo would bring together the selected guests, but the conclusion of Thomas' investigation and career in police work did not make for public celebration.

A 13-year veteran of Boulder P.D. and lead investigator for 20 months, Thomas became the face of the investigation, a position he did not want but one he believed he must take. His even teeth did not often appear in a smile. His investigation rooted him in the theory that Patsy and John Ramsey shared responsibility for JonBenet's depraved death. Before resigning from Boulder P.D., Thomas became a potential victim of blackmail or at least extortion. The *Globe*'s Craig Lewis had obtained a handful of personal family photographs from his childhood. Those photos included images of his mother, who had died by suicide.

Ultimately, Steve Thomas resigned in disgust from Boulder P.D. in August 1998 when Alex Hunter made the political decision to let a grand jury choke on the investigation his police department could not solve, especially without the assistance of the District Attorney.

As much as Lou Smit affected the acceptance of the intruder theory, Steve Thomas, handsome with a boyish face like Audie Murphy, made the case against Patsy Ramsey and John as co-conspirators in JonBenet's killing. Like Fleet White, Steve Thomas had to wear the thorned crown of the media in general and tabloids in particular as the lead detective assigned to the homicide. Thomas had a world of bizarre police experiences, humiliations, triumphs, television appearances, and a multi-million-dollar lawsuit his publisher resolved. He prospered from his tell-all true crime book, JonBenet Ramsey: Inside the Investigation, which he compiled from his official access to all the files. He received an advance of $100,000 for the book after he resigned from the Boulder Police Department, selling out to Ann Louise Bardach of *Vanity Fair,* one of the international publications of Conde Nast.

White and Thomas bonded as silenced voices, although Thomas would not be hushed despite the work of L. Lin Wood, John and Patsy's powerful civil attorney and defamation expert. Thomas' action with Conde Nast was only the first of many undisclosed settlements Wood extracted. Neither Steve Thomas nor Fleet White sacrificed their honor as they spoke to what they believed would seek justice in the face of the corruption each saw in Alex Hunter's handling of the case. Hunter's powerful political connections sealed JonBenét's memory in a tomb constructed of political tit-for-tat.

Neither man backed down. Fleet White and his family would suffer the slurs of the internet and the ignominy of becoming internet clickbait. Steve Thomas would surrender the career he loved, although the advance and royalties from his Boulder P.D. files certainly softened his landing. The former cop described himself variously as a working stiff or a carpenter

Prostitution of Justice

in the mold of Jesus of Nazareth. St. Martin's Press, as a matter of self-preservation, donated significantly to his defense as it participated in defending the defamation action for an "undisclosed settlement." Thomas' response to the conclusion of the action was, "I never paid one red cent."[48]

The flesh, blood and bone Fleet White stands out as a brave man who did not cower nor fall back to become a victim, nor would he and Priscilla sacrifice their faith, honor, or their children to the public abyss that became of John, Patsy, and Burke Ramsey. The White family has spent its post-JonBenet decades protecting their privacy, and Fleet White has protected his family and their lives like a soldier, proud, too brave to surrender, strong enough to stay in the fight or refuse to do so, depending on the demands of his conscience.

Chapter Three: Tabloid Man

Boulder is notably left but far from liberal. It is, in fact, curiously authoritarian, perhaps because of the multitudes of college students who invent all manner of "fun." Obedience to small acts of a misdemeanor nature, like overtime parking, allowing an unleashed pet, or a firecracker to mischievously explode very quickly summons the attention of Boulder P.D. The "broken windows" concept of enforcing minor infractions to dissuade more serious lawbreaking had successfully kept crime statistics low. The city had a reputation for raucous partying by the students but little violent crime. JonBenet's cruel death was the first and only homicide in 1996.

The invasion of gangs of reporters from around the nation and the world brought out an "off with their heads" attitude in both the public and police authorities. The nosy members of the press poked into the relationships between neighbors who supported the Ramseys and those who doubted them. The personal lives many wished to keep private saw their names in the news along with criminal histories, sexual preferences, reckless behavior, financial failures, or personal tragedies. The press could create doubts or sympathies by dipping into the weaknesses of human existence and, by doing so, pack their copy with more drama to spice up circulation and viewership. The citizens of Boulder, who are above average in financial resources and pride, hated the attention. In this once quirky town, overwhelmed by the interest in the JonBenet story, the intrusion of the press became as heinous as the murder itself. The cops in Boulder also had particularly good reason to feel animosity for the press.

Lead investigator Steve Thomas had a serious grudge against *Globe* editor Craig Lewis. The wily editor had obtained childhood photographs of the ex-cop's family. With a thoughtfully written note, Lewis asked if Thomas would like to have them. Not only did Thomas feel blackmailed, but also the sheer gall that a "tabloid" reporter would think to involve him in a "crime" of extortion, as he saw it, raised his blood pressure. Lewis and his editors, as writers and wordsmiths, had discussed the "safest" language for the legality of their offer. They believed that Lewis might be running close to blackmail, but by not asking for anything in return, no one crossed the line, as Lewis would not threaten the release of the family photographs. All that may have passed the smell test for the editors, but Jeff Shapiro, a *Globe*cub reporter who could have competed for the "Benedict Arnold Award" of tabloid journalism, had also tape-recorded the discussion just as he had been recording the weekly editorial meetings of his employer for several months.

Boulder is a small city. In the 2000 census, only about 95,000 persons lived there, even fewer in 1996 when the JonBenet story exploded into the headlines. Fitness, youth, and

Prostitution of Justice

beauty complemented the city, especially with a population of about 50,000 University of Colorado students who added their trendy styles while adopting the local attitudes. The University further offered a left-leaning leadership role within the student body, through the faculty and administration, and into the social fabric of the city, proscribing an unspoken demand for political and social conformity. Citizens, young and old, participated in expressing both their social and political preferences, with many competing for who could sound the most radical, not only in the classroom but beyond in boardrooms and the halls of government. And, hence, the spoof that "Boulder is twenty square miles surrounded by reality."

Pat Korton, the Ramseys' public relations man, could read the community. He applied his psychological understanding in molding public opinion to energize the community to sympathize with his clients. He squeezed the public's self-image into a bigotry that would declare a pox on all tabloids and call all journalists, print or electronic, "tabloid." To usher in this attitude of disdain, Korton staged a photo opportunity at St. John's Episcopal Church on January 5, 1997. With careful planning and invitations to the press, he created the impression that the entire congregation of the church supported the grieving parents. Ramsey's church had a congregation of wealthy, socially conscious citizens who communicated their outrage that the "press" (the same press that Pat Korton had summoned) had overrun the memorial service for JonBenet. Responding to the sensitivities of these socially conscious citizens, merchants would remove the *Globe* containing the autopsy photographs from grocery and convenience store magazine racks.

These conscientious citizens had to overlook the camera-hungry conduct of John and Patsy themselves. Suspected, with reason, of having staged the kidnap/murder of their daughter, they now paid professionals to stage their grief and their community's "support."

Niki Hayden, a writer for Boulder's *Daily Camera*, who had attended the service at St. John's on January 5, 1997, wrote an editorial about the press at the church and their invasion of a private religious service. The presence of the press tested the entire community's faith in religion and in law. Niki was accused of betraying the congregation through her editorial. When Niki talked about the editorial with the Reverend Hoverstock and warned him that John might be arrested, all the minister wanted was to keep St. John's name out of the newspaper.[49] For the most part, the citizens of Boulder knew they were safe. They realized the extraordinary peculiarity of JonBenet's death and did not expect a pedophile from a small foreign faction who would bungle a kidnapping into a murder to come creeping into their homes. What they wanted was their privacy.

Carol McKinley worked as a national reporter for Fox News after a decades-long radio career as a news reporter for

Prostitution of Justice

KOA radio in Denver, one of a few radio stations with a 50,000-watt reach. She had chummed around with reporters, cops, D.A.s, and politicians during her long career in radio before moving on to a national television opportunity. With all her contacts, she could easily unravel a bogus lead or knit together a compelling and well-documented story. The Ramsey case gave her a break from local radio to a national news reporting opportunity. She had built relationships in police departments and within the Colorado Bureau of Investigations (CBI), often scooping the competition through those decades-long relationships. Intelligent with a great sense of humor, slender, and an attractive blonde, McKinley put others at ease and made friends even more easily.

In the Ramsey case, McKinley had a home-field advantage. She had developed relationships throughout the law enforcement community and was a familiar representative of the press, in part because of her daily appearance on a trusted "news" outlet. She knew who to call, who to avoid, and how to offer that golden moment of "fame," a name or product mention to a source wanting it, or a promise of anonymity if that's what the source preferred or needed. Shrewd, outgoing, and very attractive, McKinley interviewed cops and lawyers, prosecutors, potential suspects, acquaintances, and former friends cast from Ramsey's social circle. One of those friends, Judith Phillips, had known Patsy Ramsey for over a decade way back in Atlanta and happened to have moved to Boulder shortly

Prostitution of Justice

before John and Patsy arrived. McKinley cultivated Judith Phillips like a rare orchid as an inside source.

McKinley's new work for Fox News required long hours with the spade and pickaxe. Unlike Joe Mullins or Craig Lewis of the *Globe* and other tabloid reporters, networks like NBC, CBS, and ABC, and the cable news producers did not like to dole out money for information or interviews. Reporters were expected to gather information through traditional methods by asking questions, offering a moment of on-camera fame, and giving a thank you. McKinley had plenty of good looks and charm, along with a sense of humor, but a very limited budget for the purchase of information. She resented the likes of Joe Mullins and Craig Lewis of the *Globe*, Don Gentile and David Wright of the *National Enquirer*, who often paid a thousand dollars or more for an interview and more for salacious autopsy photographs or hard evidence like sales receipts or long-distance telephone records.

McKinley and most other members of the traditional press could only buy coffee, a lunch, or a cocktail, perhaps paying a few hundred dollars for a copyrighted photograph. What McKinley did without money was develop relationships with sources, acquaintances, and potential witnesses. McKinley, like Lewis and the monied reporters, stayed in close contact with other reporters like Charlie Brennan at the *Rocky Mountain News,* Frank Coffman, a local freelancer, and any cop she could meet with, on and off the record.

Prostitution of Justice

Eventually, McKinley struck gold when Patsy's sister, Pam Paugh, began to grant her interviews. Given her inside source, McKinley could cover the inside story most reporters had missed, based not only on what the police would state, but also on her access to Pam Paugh for a unique slant on the story. While Fox News generally took the "balanced" approach of their slogan, "We report. You decide," romancing Pam Paugh became quite expensive when McKinley aired a broadcast questioning the validity of the intruder theory. The Ramseys sued her and Fox News.

By sharing information, both the traditional and tabloid press exploited the murder more effectively. With the tabloids ahead of everyone on the investigative aspect of the case, the peripheral victims of the Ramsey case—Larry Smith, Brett Sawyer, Linda Hoffman-Pugh, and others—all became fodder. Under enormous competitive pressure, tabloid reporters bought the information needed for the next deadline. They would hold their gossip until the day before they went to press, then tip a traditional reporter about the contents of the scoop for an on-air mention of when their publication with the pricey information would appear on newsstands. The tabloids could afford to spend so much money on information because they made so much money by publishing that information. The tabloid infiltration into Boulder's luxurious lifestyle spread with their corporate cards or cash, as the occasion required. No one at the tabloids worried about the public scorn laid upon the people from whom

Prostitution of Justice

they got information. Those in the traditional press who watched the tabloids scoop them every week bred unhealthy levels of professional and personal jealousy.

The jealousy and frustration also infected Boulder P.D. Tabloid reporters had purchased very private and potentially explosive information: the telephone and credit card statements of John and Patsy. Trying to gain an opening to the police investigation, the tabloids offered to assist the Boulder Police Department in its investigation by offering private information. Boulder P.D. instead asked D.A. Alex Hunter to subpoena those records, but he denied the request. The tabloids continued to buy the information with which they could smear reputations and suspects with accusations, without the wait and mess of subpoenas.

The Ramseys' lawyers quite reasonably joined the Boulder cops in despising the tabloids. Hunter, on the other hand, openly courted the attention of the press, welcoming them into his office to chitchat, hoping for generous coverage. He became especially close to Craig Lewis of the *Globe*, speaking with him almost daily. Maintaining his political alignment with Hal Haddon, Colorado's very own national power broker, Hunter would jump onto the bandwagon of Hell's Fury against the tabloids for the Ramseys, their lawyers, the cops, or anyone else who caught those rascally tabloids ferreting out damning information such as the autopsy photographs, Detective Linda

Arndt's fear of John Ramsey, or Patsy's writing of the ransom note.

Most citizens see the police as the good guys, that "thin blue line" between social order and criminal anarchy. Hollywood and television usually concur with scripts that approve of the police and portray the world of private investigations as smart, exciting, and glamorous while portraying private eyes as working for "justice" and on the same side as the cops. That, simply stated, is a false representation. In the world of reality, a state of tension exists between law enforcement and private investigators. Defense attorneys employ private eyes. As such, investigators apply their skills to reveal flaws, counterbalance, undo, and create a narrative of innocence or at least a "reasonable doubt" of guilt.

Defense investigators interview witnesses to create a narrative and evidence of innocence, not guilt. They pick apart police reports, find errors, technical or procedural, and formulate different interpretations of the facts. They testify on behalf of, rather than against, the accused. Private eyes may wear unofficial badges, but they have no powers of arrest, no threat of imprisonment, and no governmental power to pressure a suspect or witness to talk. They typically don't have court orders except to serve a subpoena, notice, or other summons to court. They can only seek the cooperation of governmental and business offices and only so far as specific statutes permit access to private information. They do not have administrative regulations with which to concern themselves. They also have a profit motive. Unlike investigative reporters, private investigators must find clients and work to pay their bills. That financial pressure provides the "bending of values" that provides false glamour in their film industry depictions.

Prostitution of Justice

Chapter Four: Tales from the Macabre

James Michael Thompson arrived in Denver as a two-year-old toddler. His father had served a career in the Navy and retired in Denver, as it turned out to be his last assignment. He now had time to spend with his family and to drink. The youngest of his children, James Michael, was a free spirit. He grew up aware of his artistic sensibilities before high school and became somewhat of a loner. He stood out. James Michael was 5'11", slender, and handsome! By the time he finished high school, he had learned to live by his good looks and his wits on Denver's Colfax Ave.

Once James Michael left home, he made money as a prostitute while hoping someday to support himself as an artist. Full of youth and wanderlust, he traveled the United States by car, train, bus, and plenty of hitchhiking. He introduced himself on the road as J.T. Colfax and adopted the moniker for when the world would recognize him as an artist. He spent time living on both the East and West coasts, exploring adventures until age began to diminish his value as a hooker, and he came home to Denver.

J.T. found work transporting corpses from morgues to mortuaries. At $13.00 a body, he could make over $100.00 in one eight-hour shift, enough to live on and drink. Usually, though, he made less. He had lived his life up and down,

Prostitution of Justice

sometimes homeless, often drunk. He knew the "Queen City of the Plains" like the back of his hand, and he knew the bars up and down Denver's Colfax Avenue from a well of memories. Thompson played one of the more pitiful sideshow performers the press found in the JonBenet Ramsey Murder Pageant. He remains best known for his chosen alias of J.T. Colfax during his few minutes of sharing JonBenet Ramsey's pitiful fame.

J.T. Colfax had begun to experiment with what he called "agit/prop" art, derived from the Russian definition of "Agitation and Propaganda." He explored photography as his medium with several of his associates in the corpse transportation business and others who prepare the dead for their final repose. They enjoyed photographing the dead and naked bodies out of their own antisocial behavior or, perhaps, fits of psychological and mental agitation. Of course, with his artistic sensibilities, J.T. would add a few words of his own "propaganda" to his photographic art.

J.T. found his expression in photographic art through the manipulation of inanimate objects (dead bodies) to make "artistic statements." Whatever J.T. Colfax believed defined his art, it violated social taboos requiring respect for the dead and risked criminal charges. Other corpse drivers had opened J.T.'s eyes to the common practice of photographing corpses. His roommate, Dave Rogers, had a sizable collection of ghastly photographs from his work in the corpse transport business.

"We all took pictures," J.T. says. "A severed head—the grosser, the better for its shock value."

With four signs on four corpses, J.T. became one of the most famous agit/prop artists in the world, thanks to the Ramsey case. The world, however, never saw his work, nor did he profit from his few creations.

Using cardboard placards attached with twine and strung to bodies, J.T. composed, to his mind, the "agitation" and "propaganda." One sign prophetically read, "Getting fired isn't the end of the world." Another corpse's sign with holiday flair read, "Happy Halloween." Perhaps running out of commentary or simply caught up in rodeo-like banter, J.T. photographed a corpse with the phrase, "Yee-Haw."

The fourth corpse in the collection was a real corker, "Jay Marvin." J.T.'s favorite talk show radio personality was Jay Marvin, whose late-night program appealed to J.T. The corpse delivery van "only had two channels on the AM radio," he explains. "I listened to The Jay Marvin Show all the time. I loved it." In fact, prior to his dismissal as a corpse deliveryman, J.T. once called in, and Jay Marvin put him on the air for half an hour while they talked about the mortuary business and corpse deliveries.

Then, on April 29, 1997, J.T. arrived at the morgue of a Boulder County Hospital. He arrived at about midnight to transport a corpse to Monarch Mortuary in Denver. At about the

Prostitution of Justice

same time, a man from an eye clinic arrived to harvest the eyes from that very same corpse, and J.T. would have to wait. Time would be taken from J.T. That irritated him. He had needs, and he couldn't make deliveries or money while he waited. He was also drunk, another perk he enjoyed in his solitary employment. Now, having already used mouthwash to disguise his breath, he had to wait until the eyes were harvested before he could get another drink.

But then, J.T. found something to give him a "Yee-Haw." JonBenet Ramsey's corpse was the most renowned dead body in Colorado, the United States, and the world. She'd been right there in that very morgue. Her autopsy photographs had been bought, sold, and even banned in Boulder months earlier. The controversy over the release of her autopsy photographs impressed those in the cadaver business as media hype and silliness, given their familiarity with "agitprop" imagery. Bored, angry, and drunk, J.T. took the pages of the hospital log containing the entry about JonBenet's arrival.

J.T. left the hospital with the corpse, its eyes harvested, and his little piece of JonBenet memorabilia. He knew what to do with the corpse but had to think about the memorabilia. After some sleep, he set about making multiple copies of the morgue log. With a sense of accomplishment, fame, and bravado, he mailed many of those copies to people he knew around the country. He sent the original pages from his petty theft to a friend in San Francisco, California, for safekeeping. By then,

Prostitution of Justice

he thought that the political paralysis in Boulder had reduced JonBenet's death into a morbid joke. J.T. also had no care for the Ramseys. All the same, he asked the same friend in San Francisco to mail the original document back, anonymously, to an East Colfax Avenue bar in Denver J.T. had frequented.

Excited about his find but not yet knowing what "agitation" he could create with it, he had neither the corpse of the little girl to photograph nor any idea for the document's use as "propaganda." He also found himself down on his luck and not making enough money transporting corpses. "I was broke," J.T. explained. To make matters worse, J.T. attempted to shoplift a roll of processed film of corpses from the grocery store he used for developing and printing.

Security moved in and busted him for shoplifting. When the police arrived and opened the envelope containing the photographs of his taboo creations, "That was the biggest freak show ever!"[50] Colfax said. Homicide detectives from Denver and Arapahoe County swarmed J.T. "Who are these dead people? Why did you put signs on them?" The cops, wanting a confession and using a common law enforcement fib, claimed that they were not interested in prosecuting him for shoplifting or, later, abuse of a corpse. They just wanted to save the family members of the deceased from any grief or horror. In the first hours of questioning, the police wondered if they had found a serial murderer, one who killed people to turn them into taboo art through a macabre imagination and freedom of speech.

Prostitution of Justice

To the disappointment of cold case and serial crimes investigators, J.T. Colfax's story checked out. He had a menial job supporting his art by transporting dead bodies that were legally obtained and properly logged. He was released on a personal recognizance bond for the shoplifting. To his misfortune, things had soured considerably in his personal life. Only a few friends knew about the pilfered morgue pages, and an important friend included J.T.'s roommate, Dave Rogers.

Of course, M & M Transport Company fired him as the publicity from the discovery of his corpse photographs and the shoplifting surfaced. More immediately, Dave Rogers did not want J.T. at his home anymore. The risk for Rogers was far too great with the collection of corpse photographs he possessed and with the police ever so very curious about any photographs Rogers may have taken of corpses when they questioned him. Rogers helped J.T. load his few possessions into a car and then dumped him and his bags on the curb outside the Denver YMCA.

Through the cruelty of age, J.T.'s desirable youth and good looks had faded. To pay the rent, he now took day work beginning at 7:00 a.m. at minimum wage, doing hard labor for Manpower, Inc. He also had numerous and frequent court dates. The City and County of Denver had jurisdiction where the shoplifting occurred and required his attendance downtown. Arapahoe County, beyond walking distance, took jurisdiction because of where J.T. had taken the photographs for several

Prostitution of Justice

counts of Abuse of a Corpse. Each jurisdiction also required that J.T. make and keep appointments with Pretrial Services, and these separate authorities required drug testing on such a regular basis that J.T. could not obtain or hold a steady job.

It was after one of his long, hard, sweaty days that J.T. sat relaxing in the YMCA community room. He watched the early evening news and sipped a forbidden beer. Pretrial services did not permit the consumption of alcohol. He learned from the broadcast that Boulder P.D. was investigating some missing morgue pages in the JonBenet Ramsey case. He surmised then that his friend, former roommate, and fellow artist, Dave Rogers, had dropped a dime on him.

According to J.T., a reporter for the *Denver Post*, Mike O'Keefe, contacted him the day after the newscast. The reporter explained that he had received a phone call from an "unnamed source" about the JonBenet Ramsey case. O'Keefe somehow learned that he could contact J.T. at the YMCA. When he first received the call, J.T. asked the reporter if he was a cop. O'Keefe calmed J.T. and convinced him that he really was a newspaper reporter. J.T. Colfax, the fledgling Agit/Prop artist, could feel his world falling away beneath him. Any trouble he found himself in for his artwork amounted to nothing compared to the disaster he saw colliding with his world now.

J.T. could not return the original pages from the morgue log. They were too "hot" to keep in his personal possession, so he sent them to a friend in San Francisco "for safekeeping."

Prostitution of Justice

However, his friend on the West Coast wanted nothing to do with JonBenet Ramsey's morgue logs. Instead of engaging in J.T.'s risk-taking, the friend mailed the originals back to a bar in Denver on Colfax Avenue, which he believed J.T. still frequented. J.T. put his face in his hands. Who knew where the logs were anymore? He wished he could just explain the whole fiasco to someone—anyone. To J.T.'s misfortune, the closest "anyone" turned out to be a newspaper reporter.

Flattered by the attention but not calculating the risk of discussing his behavior with the press, J.T. invited O'Keefe to accompany him to the Denver Public Library. They walked to the library, located only a few blocks from J.T.'s room at the YMCA. There, in the Vietnam section, the Agit/Prop artist had hidden his photocopies of the stolen morgue pages and gave the reporter a copy. In an ordinary murder case, O'Keefe would have taken little interest in some missing morgue pages. This, of course, was no ordinary case. This was the JonBenet Ramsey case. The story had legs that reached around the world! Anything unusual or kinky sold newspapers. Of course, upon receipt of the morgue logs, O'Keefe contacted the Boulder P.D. He had a tip to offer and, maybe by ingratiating himself, Boulder P.D. may leak something juicy to O'Keefe in the future. Besides, maybe J.T. was the murderer? Maybe he wanted a souvenir? Maybe a *Denver Post* reporter could gain fame by helping to solve the JonBenet Ramsey case? The police were not far behind the reporter.

Prostitution of Justice

"I've been expecting you," J.T. recalls saying to Boulder Detectives Steve Thomas and Dan Gossage when they appeared at his door at the YMCA. J.T. confessed immediately to pilfering the morgue pages listing the arrival of JonBenet's corpse but truthfully denied any involvement in the murder and torture.

The detectives only questioned J.T. briefly, then handcuffed him for transport to Boulder, where hours of serious interrogation would take place. Once at headquarters, Gossage took hair and saliva samples. J.T.'s ignorance of details did not impress his captors with his innocence before locking J.T. in a holding cell. He would wait there for a polygraph test. The detectives offered him no choice but to take the test, although it was his right to refuse. He had no lawyer and, thus, no knowledge of the limitations on police requests or demands.

"You could see the greed in their eyes," J.T. says of the cops. "They thought they had JonBenet's killer."

J.T. knew he had become the leading suspect in the JonBenet Ramsey murder, and he also knew that being innocent wouldn't necessarily result in one's freedom. He had also learned long ago that a poor, white, homosexual without a lawyer needed help, and the help would come from the office of an overworked and usually uninspired public defender's office. Along with the greed he saw, J.T. could also feel repugnance from the cops. He was on his own and knew he

Prostitution of Justice

couldn't count on any help if the authorities wanted to hold him in jail for a long time.

Once the detectives tossed him into the general population, now all locked up and hardened by experience, J.T. relaxed some. Knowing he had never even thought of murdering anyone, ever, especially a child, he felt safer among the inmates than with detectives. Now, not so frightened but always a little bored, he wished he could just go back to work chauffeuring corpses, just listening to The Jay Marvin Show. At that moment, he became inspired. It occurred to him to call The Jay Marvin Show from the jail.

J.T. had to wait some time to get access to the pay phone that all the inmates relied upon to reach out of jail, but it was worth it. Jay Marvin, who was not a fool, found himself on top of the red-hottest story in the world, live, now, on his program, with a prime suspect behind bars in the JonBenet murder case!

The switchboard at the radio station began to smoke. Next, the switchboard at the jail caught fire. J.T. told of his shoddy treatment by Boulder P.D., wondering if his civil rights had been violated and expressing his innocence. Jay Marvin, a sympathetic listener and showman, had given out the Boulder County Jail's phone number on air. This permitted his listeners to ask the keepers why J.T. Colfax had to cool it in jail. Why wasn't he permitted to see a lawyer? Why was he being questioned without a lawyer?

Prostitution of Justice

Hoping to put out a public relations fire, "the jailhouse brass showed up," J.T. recalled. They demanded to know if he had used the only telephone in the holding cell to call The Jay Marvin Show. J.T. sputtered into laughter, "Well, duh?" One of the problems that plagued the Ramsey case was not only police incompetence but also the fact that that incompetence would sparkle when Boulder P.D. or the Sheriff's Office began asking questions long after facts had revealed the answer.

The JonBenet Ramsey case did not bring about the arrest of J.T. Colfax. The man's poor judgment, fascination with the macabre, hunger for artistic recognition, and an unusual, if not perverted, sense of humor did. Once he came under the big top of the JonBenet Ramsey Murder Pageant, he found himself in the center ring like a clown as he was shot out of a cannon. The Jay Marvin show opened the door for the public to discuss the disparate treatment of the ragged J.T. Colfax compared to well-healed and better-lawyered John and Patsy Ramsey. Facts, after all, had not led Boulder P.D. to find the body of a mutilated child in J.T. Colfax's room or the basement of the YMCA. It took a confession to reveal he had swiped a couple of "official" sheets of paper related to the national scandal in Boulder.

Now in the running for a ratings touchdown, the Jay Marvin Show began a radiothon to help raise bail for the beleaguered J.T. Colfax. Next, Marvin contacted one of the most prominent criminal defense lawyers in Denver to represent the implausible murderer of JonBenet Ramsey, none

Prostitution of Justice

other than Harvey Steinberg. Even though the kind of horsepower Steinberg brought to a courtroom didn't come cheap, the JonBenet Ramsey case brought with it worldwide publicity and a pro bono legal defense.

Having cut his teeth in criminal defense work at the Arapahoe County Public Defender's Office, Steinberg's talent, once in the private market, earned him enormous retainers far outside the reach of the guests of the Y.M.C.A. Steinberg often represented big-name bad-boy athletes such as former Denver Bronco Bill Romanowski of Superbowl fame, Pro Bowl Bronco Brandon Marshall, and Stanley Cup goalie Patrick Roy of the Colorado Avalanche.[51] He earned his well-deserved reputation as a tough, relentless criminal defense lawyer and brass knuckles master of cross-examination. He didn't have to go to trial often because prosecutors did not like the embarrassment and headlines when he won trials. With court dates always jammed and deputy district attorneys wanting plea bargains, prosecutors considered him "high maintenance." He cut the deals clients could live with. Prosecutors knew the embarrassment Steinberg administered in the alternative when prosecutors got cocky or thought to enhance their reputation. Every case Steinberg handled carried the potential of being a stone loser for the D.A. who challenged him at trial.

When Boulder P.D. realized J.T. had not murdered anyone but did produce embarrassing headlines for the embattled department thanks to the stunt on the Jay Marvin

Prostitution of Justice

show, they cut him loose with a charge of petty theft. The new charges in Boulder came as no big deal but rather as a sense of relief given how close he had come to a legal guillotine with the JonBenet Ramsey murder.

J.T. understood he had publicly embarrassed the jail and its staff. That felt pretty good for a veteran of incarceration. He made a lot of friends at the Boulder County Jail with his call to the Jay Marvin Show. Marvin snagged the day's ratings jackpot for his on-air interview with a genuine JonBenet Ramsey suspect. The *Denver Post* reporter, Mike O'Keefe, got his scoop for finding the purloined pages. Thomas and Gossage got a collar, maybe not much of a collar in the universe of the JonBenet Ramsy Murder Pageant. Still, they took heart by taking a "bad guy" off the streets. The law firm of Springer & Steinberg got a little free press. Unfortunately for J.T., his run-in with the Ramsey case had only just begun. Life would get tougher.

J.T. recalls that Harvey Steinberg seemed just plain bored when they met to undertake the defense of only a misdemeanor charge. The prize for representing JonBenet's murderer didn't materialize. After the radio show, the headlines grew less rewarding: "Necrophilia, Homosexual, Prostitute." Steinberg had stepped in, pro bono, to defend the rights of J.T. Now, the super lawyer had become a character in a radio stunt. All the same, J.T., never having been represented by a private attorney like Steinberg, felt safe in the hands of a person with

Prostitution of Justice

that level of skill. What J.T. needed, which Steinberg did not have to offer, was substance abuse treatment and possibly mental health counseling.

One afternoon, while still under court supervision, J.T. took the bus from Denver to Boulder to visit the abandoned Ramsey mansion at 755 15th St. He had a lot on his mind. He couldn't make enough money as a day laborer to pay his rent, eat, and pay bus fares to and from the drug testing mandated by pretrial services, nor for the seemingly ceaseless court dates and police interviews.

His troubles from the morgue pages stoked his curiosity about the murder and about JonBenet herself. He wandered around to the back of the Ramsey home, onto the patio, and pulled out a chair to sit and meditate on his broken hopes at the table. There, he watched the approaching sunset, contemplating the horrible death of JonBenet, all the mystery surrounding the murder, and his Boulder case, along with the other cases in Arapahoe County. He felt like a wad of chewed gum. The media had sucked all the sweetness from his story as he sat hungry, homeless, and now deeply saddened by his circumstances and especially the death of the six-year-old beauty princess.

J.T. had been sitting on the patio of the former Ramsey house for a couple of hours, ruminating against the society he lived in, the mansion of the Ramseys, and the homelessness he now experienced. His depression moved him to make his next bad decision. He walked around the house to the front door,

Prostitution of Justice

where he noticed the mail slot and some old mail stuffed into the slot that had not dropped inside the house. It was just junk mail, nothing of value. After pawing through it, he pulled out a nearly empty disposable lighter and lit a cigarette. Glancing at the mail, he took an advertising flyer, set it on fire, and stuffed the flaming paper through the slot, then some more of the junk mail. He didn't expect, nor hope, nor believe that the whole house would catch on fire. By now, his cheap lighter was empty, and his matches were used up. He shrugged his shoulders and wandered away to a pay phone, where he called Boulder P.D. and snitched on himself for committing the arson. Of course, in accordance with Boulder P. D.'s usual malaise, an investigation must be done before contacting the confessor, before a transient could be arrested and provided free room and board at the county jail.

Some of that malaise arose from a "gun shy" attitude within Boulder P.D. regarding anything Ramsey. First, the authorities contacted Ramsey's attorneys for permission to check out the property for signs of arson. Once Boulder P.D. received the grant of permission, responding officers found the propped-open mail slot, burned matches, a disposable cigarette lighter, and some ashes. Their discoveries gave them probable cause, that requirement so elusive in the JonBenet murder case, for a felony arson charge. This time, Boulder P.D. had confidence that they knew who did it. The only problem, and problems always confounded the Ramsey case: the man who confessed to the arson was J.T. Colfax, who, by now, they had lost track of.

During the time that Boulder P.D. conducted its investigation, J.T. had wandered away from the tony neighborhood of the Ramseys to find a park bench in Boulder close to Boulder Creek. The next morning, his body cold and stiff from intermittent sleep outdoors, J.T. called the Boulder Police Department to confess a second time. This time, Detective Steve Thomas arrested him just west of Boulder's Pearl Street Mall. The D.A.'s office, satisfied with a confession, found probable cause to approve charges of arson, a serious felony. J.T.'s search for unanswerable questions outside captivity ended. Harvey Steinberg withdrew, and the court assigned J.T. a public defender. If J.T. thought Steinberg seemed bored, J.T.'s new lawyer, Cary Lacklin, was, well, "a bastard."

Whatever Lacklin learned in law school about the zealous defense of his clients lost its shine under the policy of easy plea bargains and a preference for no trials in D.A. Hunter's Boulder Courthouse. The monotonous complaints of his clients, culprits sometimes claiming innocence and, worse yet, demanding a dismissal or a trial, possibly soured Lacklin. J.T. found Lacklin to be a "sourpuss," which is the kindest description the luckless arsonist had of his lawyer.

Now realizing, but not respecting, the amount of trouble he had brewed for himself, J.T.'s antipathy for his lawyer did

Prostitution of Justice

little to minimize the potential for a long sentence behind bars. Fortunately, J.T. had not burned anything with fraudulent intent, nor caused thousands of dollars in damages, nor was anyone injured. He met the elements of a misdemeanor arson charge. All the same, with days of his life draining like so many grains of sand in an hourglass while in jail, J.T. set upon a correspondence campaign to the judge presiding over his case. In a series of letters, J.T. pleaded for another lawyer, any lawyer, other than Cary Lacklin. Of course, the judge who observed Lacklin's professionalism every day in his courtroom had no sympathy for the arsonist's plight. Like a foreman in a hog farm, cleaning up after the livestock was not his job. In fact, J.T. Colfax's experience identifies a common complaint of clients who must accept a public defender or try a "do-it-yourself" defense, most often resulting in a finding of guilty.

No one really cared if J.T. had a lawyer or a reluctant bureaucrat who didn't care whom he represented. Lacklin didn't care that his client hated him. Few people open dusty old court files to read the complaints of convicted arsonists about their dissatisfaction with their legal representation, their inhumane treatment, and especially the poverty that holds them in a cage. J.T. Colfax's file is a work of art on the failure of the American criminal justice system and its catastrophic effects on the poor.

Lacklin didn't want to talk about J.T. Colfax. He responded to inquiries about his representation of J.T. in a dour monotone with all the humanity of a corpse wearing a sign that

Prostitution of Justice

reads, Drop Dead. Lacklin just didn't give a damn about the years J.T. would spend in jail through his easy-deal representation over befuddled objections. He didn't return J.T.'s calls made to him from the jail. He consistently failed to meet his client in person to discuss any aspect of the case outside the urgent moment of the courtroom. J.T. says Lacklin misled him about his rights and his legal options. This tragic character's clearest memory of Lacklin is watching him "walk hand in hand from the courtroom" with prosecutor Trip DeMuth at each court appearance. "They were working on the same team to put me in prison!"

The problematic case, given J.T.'s admissions and outbursts with his public defender in court and five angry letters documenting his court file, did not land him at the top of a bureaucratic heap of concern. At one hearing, J.T. asked the judge to put Lacklin in jail for repeatedly lying to him.

"Not today. Maybe later," the judge responded.

The judge remained unsympathetic to J.T.'s requests. Lacklin pushed a plea of guilty, refusing to take the case to trial, even though, in theory, the decision to go to trial goes to the defendant. Now guilty of attempted arson, the authorities washed their hands and abandoned him to a long stay behind bars. In his own way, J.T. would not "go gently into that good night," to quote Dylan Thomas; rather, J.T. "raged against the dying of the light."

Prostitution of Justice

The incompetent arsonist took up a long-term residence in the Boulder County Jail. Always prone to act in the face of boredom, he began to "rage" through correspondence. He mailed postcards and letters to newspapers describing the various violations of civil rights or unsanitary conditions of his environment. Sometimes, his missives would find publication. That caused the jailhouse brass to give him "vacations," as J.T. describes his relocations to other county jails around the state. He would enjoy the time outside his cell for travel to rural county lockups. The new environments did not stop him from identifying or claiming to have identified similar code violations at his new residence. The dislocations did cause his mail to reach him sporadically, if at all. Many of his letters to the editors of newspapers "disappeared." J.T. would rewrite the missive and have another inmate send it. He developed a theory that JonBenet was murdered by an attendee at a party that was going on in the neighborhood that fateful night. Some of his correspondence found its way to eager publication in Denver's Westword, along with other local news outlets in his temporary county of residence.

The plea bargain reached between Lacklin and prosecutor Trip DeMuth resulted in J.T.'s serving a full two years for a criminal attempt in the arson fiasco, concurrent with convictions for criminal mischief and petty theft. He received credit for good behavior but no credit for the seven months of

Prostitution of Justice

time he served while begging for a different lawyer. He walked out of jail on Bastille Day, July 14, 1999, a free man, sort of. During his August 2001 interview at a photo studio in Boulder, J.T. said, "I still live like I'm in jail."[52] He sat with a worn-out look, his shoulders slumped, his eyes full of time and sadness. As his interview came to its end, the weight of his involvement in the JonBenet Ramsey case bore down on J.T.: "Except for movies and cigarettes, there's no difference. I don't feel safe. I don't know if I'll ever feel safe again. I try never to leave my apartment except to go to work. I'm a bartender, and I work in the same building where I have my apartment. All I do is save money. I want to buy a house in Scranton, Pennsylvania. It's the cheapest place in the country to buy a house. Maybe I'll feel safe there."[53]

The photographer, Judith Phillips, documented in black and white images many of the Ramsey celebrities and bit players of the saga. During his time in the photo studio, J.T. Colfax offered his story to the author in what seemed like a cathartic act. Before he left, he brought out a not badly damaged page torn from a spiral notebook, read it, and gave it to Judith Phillips:

"Something has changed in me.

My view of Boulder has been shattered.

I'm not a vegetarian, but I do like to recycle my beer cans.

Prostitution of Justice

Now, that doesn't even seem to be "hip" anymore.

I would like to see a memorial for JonBenet.

A friend told me that a bench with a plaque (IN LOVING MEMORY) was placed in Chautauqua Park. I went up there and looked but couldn't find it.

I would like a place to leave flowers and mourn for JonBenet.

I want to see her remembered for the many positive things about her.

I have celebrated JonBenet's birthday (Aug. 6) for the last two years now.

She would be nine years old today."[54]

Prostitution of Justice

Chapter Five: Rent

Linda Hoffman-Pugh cleaned house, did laundry, handled chores, and helped Patsy with the children. When police investigators first contacted her at her home at 7:00 p.m. on December 26, 1996, to tell her of JonBenet's murder, she screamed and began to shake uncontrollably. The police took handwriting samples and grilled her for three-and-a-half hours.[55] John and Patsy had named her as a suspect.

Before being accused of murder, Linda Hoffman-Pugh and her husband, Merv, had earned their status as veterans of the working class. Merv worked in construction, weather permitting, and drank too much beer. He struggled to read the ransom note when freelance reporter Frank Coffman showed it to him. He had to ask Coffman for the pronunciations and meanings of some words in the note. Linda, heavyset, bent from years of manual labor, asked for the meaning of the word "hence."

On December 23, 1996, two days before the murder, the housekeeper asked Patsy to loan her $2,000 that she desperately needed to catch up on her rent. Patsy granted the request, expanding the trust in the relationship through her act of charity. The loan put a strain on Linda's family during the Christmas season, and she carried her hard work to the wealthy home with even more dedication by bringing Merv and her daughter to the house to assist her with the increased Christmas duties. The loan raised the cleaning woman's self-esteem as a trusted maid. She did not have the social status to join the family and guests for the watch party while waiting for a kidnapper's call.

Despite her ostentatious warmth and accommodating southern charm in dealing with servants, Patsy regarded them as dispensable, especially when the police asked her to name possible suspects. While John and Patsy Ramsey could afford to hire the silk-stocking law firm of Haddon, Morgan, and Foreman, private eyes, a world-famous profiler, and a crisis management public relations specialist, Linda Hoffman-Pugh and Merv could barely afford food and shelter. Linda Hoffman-Pugh made a wonderful, defenseless "suspect."

Linda Hoffman-Pugh knew of JonBenet's bedwetting and fecal soiling. She had to pull the sheets and do the laundry to clean up after JonBenet. Patsy knew that Linda had intimate knowledge of her daughter's least attractive behavior. Through pride, fear, or denial, Patsy sought to demean Linda, who had too much credibility as an insider. A needy housekeeper in debt to Patsy and John could offer viable kidnapper and murder suspects by including Linda's husband, Merv, and their children in the package of "a small foreign faction."

In the early hours of the police investigation, the woman who washed the linen revealed the frequency of JonBenet's bedwetting. Linda noted that the problem had been ongoing and that the child had begun soiling her linens with feces. Patsy asserts in *The Death of Innocence* that the bedwetting did not bother her, asking, reasonably, if a woman who had survived the most serious stages of cancer would find wet sheets so great a concern that she would murder her child.[56]

Patsy makes a valid comparison. The issue of fecal soiling presents a more disconcerting problem than JonBenet's bedwetting. That the information came from a servant doesn't describe full disclosure. More disturbing for those familiar with the symptoms of serious acts of pedophilia is that a child who soils her bed linen with feces is an indicator of sexual child abuse, as the child tries to make herself less attractive to the perpetrator. Frequently soiled linen with feces represents a common response of a sexually abused child. The excrement serves as a defense against the intrusion of their bodies to make themselves undesirable in a situation under which they have no control.

Once Linda Hoffman-Pugh understood that the Ramseys had not only abandoned her as their trusted employee but had fingered her in JonBenet's murder, the press found a willing source of information from inside the Ramsey home. The Ramseys had circled the wagons, insisting that their "friends" must not speak to reporters. Like a jilted lover, Hoffman-Pugh looked forward to gossiping about her former employer, the one she thought to be her friend, while the one who would also throw her to the wolves.

Prostitution of Justice

No matter the soiling by JonBenet, Linda Hoffman-Pugh cared deeply for JonBenet. She wanted the murderer identified, caught, and prosecuted. Confused by the Ramseys, perhaps her information would identify the murderer, explain the kinky exploitation of JonBenet, or conversely, lead the authorities to affirm the innocence of John and Patsy. If that bit of tabloid gossip pointed instead to the guilt of the already suspected parents, karma would come full circle.

Before the expiration of the housekeeper's 15 minutes of fame, the public expected an arrest. Such a graphic murder with obscene and titillating details had ushered forth a public cry for justice with an undertone demanding revenge. The arrest of John and Patsy would have surprised a few earlier in the investigation, including Linda Hoffman-Pugh. The faithful housekeeper remained loyal to Patsy Ramsey for a long time after the murder. It took the publication of Lawrence Schiller's *Perfect Murder, Perfect Town* in 1999 for her to learn that Patsy had fingered her for the murder.

The loyal housekeeper considered Patsy to be a wonderful mother. She admitted that she didn't know John as well. She thought of him as cold, a distant figure in the household, but she had little interaction with him. Except for the bedwetting and the feces, Linda noticed little unusual behavior in JonBenet's behavior. JonBenet could sass and was spoiled, naturally, but Hoffman-Pugh saw JonBenet as a bright, beautiful, and affectionate child, as did everyone else. In fact, the housekeeper's youngest child and JonBenet were playmates.

Hoffman-Pugh's positive public statements about the Ramseys as parents and Patsy as an affectionate mother didn't keep her on the list of "friends." She had spoken to the police, which was normal under the circumstances, but she had all that "inside" knowledge that made her unreliable and not to be trusted. The cold shoulder came easily once the Ramseys abandoned the home on 15th Street, and they had no further need for a maid in Boulder. Linda wondered why the woman she worshipped as her friend and employer had not called her for comfort. Patsy hadn't even mailed her a note.

A year later, in December 1997, a producer for Geraldo Rivera's show, familiar with Lawrence Schiller's book, asked Linda if she knew that both Patsy and Patsy's mother, Nedra, had named her as a potential suspect for the murder. A year after the death, Linda Hoffman-Pugh realized her former friend, employer, and benefactor had betrayed her. Still suffering the awful crush of the embarrassment of being named as a suspect on nationwide television, Linda began to rethink her loyalty to Patsy. Not better prepared but certainly better informed, she opened her eyes and looked at her family's financial needs. She began to cash in on her insider's knowledge of the Ramsey household. Now, she would talk about the times she had seen JonBenet fuss about being the little beauty princess or how the little girl would address the housekeeper disrespectfully. Linda had little interest in the press until she had been "dismissed." In response, the Ramseys denied her statements about the dynamics of the household. Some claimed that tabloid money bribed the former housekeeper to disparage their perfectly normal home.

In time, Linda did acquire a little of the media's money. She accepted thousands of dollars from the American Journal, the *National Enquirer*, the *Globe*, Geraldo Rivera, and any others with a checkbook. She paid the rent quite a few times, but her story aged. Patsy could give her nothing new. Linda's story and opinions grew more and more meaningless to the press as the public relations machine of John and Patsy ground her up. *The Death of Innocence* would identify the housekeeper as one of a crowd of likely child killers the couple kept.

Linda did not fall neatly into the snare of the Ramsey defense once summoned to the grand jury. Her story would have ended in silence at the grand jury if not for the intervention of victim rights attorney Darnay Hoffman. The New York City lawyer and victim's rights advocate had represented Bernard Goetz, New York City's "Subway Vigilante." In November 1997, Hoffman filed a civil action directing Alex Hunter's office to file charges against John and Patsy Ramsey under an old and little-used Colorado statute. The Ramseys dismissed Hoffman as a publicity hound.

Hoffman, nevertheless, pursued the release of

Prostitution of Justice

information on the little Colorado Beauty Princess's murder He continued to press his representation of Hoffman-Pugh based on her First Amendment right to speak publicly about her grand jury testimony. The case eventually wound its way through to the U.S. District Court. There, Judge Wiley Daniel ruled on July 5, 2001, that Linda had the right to speak.

Linda Hoffman-Pugh's grand jury testimony focused on Patsy Ramsey, as did much of the grand jury investigation. She believed that Patsy was complicit in JonBenet's death. In this claim, the law protected her from the kind of lawsuit filed by the Ramseys against Steve Thomas for stating his beliefs in his book. The difference is that Linda had made her statements under oath in courtroom testimony, which is protected speech. Linda also had no book royalties or personal wealth. The Ramseys and their legal advisors could find no profit in a lawsuit. Linda Hoffman-Pugh was also a loose cannon whose utterances could only muddy the waters of John and Patsy's claim of innocence.

Linda Hoffman-Pugh may have paid a few more months of rent, but for others who would suggest parental involvement, the Ramseys' legal team handled the brigades of lean, hungry reporters who stepped too far with a costly summons to court to "Shut Up!" Even if an accuser had deep pockets of money, patience, and strength to fight, the lawsuits had to settle. The lawyer in the civil action and his clients could meekly claim a shallow victory for "truth" under the terms of the sealed settlement. Steve Thomas,

Prostitution of Justice

the author of his historically significant *JonBenet Ramsey: Inside the Ramsey Murder Investigation*, says he never paid the Ramseys a "dime" in any settlement, and that is good for him. His publisher, St. Martin's Press, paid plenty to defend Thomas and itself while the terms of the settlement said nothing.

The bitter truth of JonBenet's sick and violent death remains in sealed grand jury records, sealed civil settlements, and a wall of silence in fear of being sued. Thus, the truth, or the search for it, dies in finding "justice" for JonBenet Ramsey. Hal Haddon, mastermind of the ingenious strategy to silence leaks and the press through grand jury proceedings, had worked before in his handling of the Rocky Flats plutonium poisoning scandal in the late 1980s. Haddon defended Rockwell International. Rules 6.2 and
6.3 of the Colorado Rules of Criminal Procedure forbid witnesses at grand jury proceedings from discussing their testimony. Haddon engineered the passage of that rule in 1998, while Alex Hunter held up the investigation before summoning a grand jury.

Whatever Hoffman-Pugh may have wanted to tell the public about her grand jury questions or testimony, Colorado's Revised Statutes were silenced, as were all the other witnesses. However, on November 19, 2002, almost six years after the Christmas tragedy of 1996, Linda Hoffman-Pugh achieved a courthouse victory. Silenced for years under a very real threat of imprisonment for contempt of court, Hoffman-Pugh's story and courtroom testimony came to light. Of course, the intruder theory had taken root, the press had moved on, and the safe bet was to call the Ramseys innocent until proven guilty, a claim that would never go to trial nor create a story worth paying a housekeeper's rent.

Prostitution of Justice

Chapter Six: Information Brokers

In January 1997, a caller who identified himself only as "John" contacted McGucken Hardware in Boulder. John wanted to know about two American Express charges his wife, Patsy Ramsey, had made on their credit card. The caller followed up days later with a letter signed "John Ramsey" requesting the release of the receipts.

James Rapp and his wife, Regana, worked as information brokers for private parties. Rapp began his training as a private investigator after his conviction for car theft. He served time for a parole violation, where he honed his talents as a liar. Since Colorado had no licensing laws for private investigators, Rapp found a new profession and a promising market for his skills, knowledge, and brass. He repossessed autos, performed difficult process service, and, especially, filched private information over the phone, using his talent for lying. He began selling his services as an information broker in the Denver area in the late 1980s. He trained others in the cons used to trick information from sources and built up a nationwide clientele in time for reporters who covered the JonBenet Ramsey murder investigation and freak show.

Prostitution of Justice

Rapp and his staff conned anyone—public, private, or business—answering the telephone into providing unpublished telephone numbers, bank account records, credit card statements, long-distance records, and even social employment traces. He then sold the information to private investigators. Many of the gumshoes he sold his services to were former FBI or NCIS intelligence officers and a few journalists. Few had the kind of criminal training Rapp did, nor the gall to work his scams over the telephone. Rapp could impersonate a woman so believably that men, playing into Rapp's coy telephone sexuality, would offer any information for which he asked. "My husband and I never have sex anymore," he might tease. "I think he's having an affair." Rapp would then ask for a copy of credit card records, which were mailed to a post office box, adding, "My husband doesn't know about it."

Pinkerton's, Inc. and its agents coined the phrase "pretext" after the time of the Civil War. The investigator pretends to be a person with a right to the information or simply a person with an appropriate curiosity who asks a source for otherwise private information. Most private investigators have used and still use pretexts to garner information, but few develop the techniques and level of artistry that James Rapp did. Private investigators who used this kind of calculated guile very rarely encountered any repercussions.

A lawyer may not use a pretext in his own investigations. The Colorado Rules of Professional Conduct, the rules that govern lawyers in Colorado, prohibit a lawyer and his employees or agents from using theft, fraud, deception, or misrepresentation. That made the kind of information Rapp developed in the Ramsey case valuable, a hair's breadth removed from attorney discipline.

Working under the names Touchtone Investigations, Dirty Deeds Done Dirt Cheap, and Phantom Investigations, Rapp would uncover an unpublished phone number by calling customer service at the local cable TV business office, the daily newspaper, or the local pizza delivery company—anybody who would have the target's personal phone number. Posing as an angry husband, he talked service representatives into turning over long-distance telephone records. Acting as John Ramsey, he obtained credit card and hardware store records. He drove the Boulder Police Department crazy by providing those records to the tabloids and offering his assistance to the humiliated police.

That Rapp preyed on the innocent and the guilty, reaping profits from fictional identities he created, posing as the legitimate credit card owner or troubled clients, and identifying himself as anyone but himself over the telephone, did not bother his clients, mostly private investigators. Occasionally, Rapp erred. Relying on his information during a deposition called to expose a debtor, it turned out he had "imagined" a stock brokerage account that did not exist. He lost his client, Investigative Reporting Services, Inc., and the private

Prostitution of Justice

investigative agency lost a profoundly disappointed client over the expense of the investigation and a deposition.[57]

Rapp realized the value of information and his talent for obtaining it. He billed by the hour, as most private investigators do, plus expenses. In the early years, he charged for made-up long-distance charges on his invoice and billed for hours of work he had accomplished in minutes. Occasionally, he made up information to make it more "interesting" and give a reason for the time it took to gather so painstakingly.[58]

Robert Brown had worked in law enforcement and as a private investigator all his adult life. Later in his career, he partnered in the firm Brown & Cracraft for several years before deciding to finish off his career and return to a steady government paycheck at the Colorado Bureau of Investigation. While Robert Brown and his partner, Jane Cracraft, a retired *Denver Post* reporter, had concentrated on criminal defense work, both knew the value of pretexts in criminal defense and civil work. They knew James Rapp and others like him. When they needed help, and they did not know how to develop the information by a simple pretext or other traditional means, an information broker could often crack the case, and the private investigator just passed along the cost in a final invoice.

Rapp grew increasingly brazen as his company prospered. Eventually, he came under the scrutiny of serious players in law enforcement, but no thanks to the circus going on in Boulder. Agent Brown, having returned to the law

Prostitution of Justice

enforcement community at the CBI, led the information-brokering investigation. Craig Lewis and Joe Mullins of the *Globe* had used the hardware store data obtained by Rapp for a lurid story about the binding of JonBenet. When the *Globe* published, Boulder police stood mortified once again.

The massacre at Columbine High School in the Denver suburb of Littleton occurred on April 20, 1999. Reporters had continued camping out in motels along the front range of the Rocky Mountains, still trying to unpack the mysterious handling of JonBenet's fake kidnapping, torture, and murder. Suddenly, the worldwide press corps found a fresh story with national reporters already present only a few dozen miles north in Boulder.

James Rapp had become a staple for a few editors who could authorize juicy payments for juicy information. He raked in business during the initial days of the first slaughter in a plague of mass school shootings at Columbine High School in Littleton, Colorado, on April 20, 1999. Rapp provided hungry reporters with the phone numbers of family members of Columbine victims. The insensitive press used the information to call the bereaved. The anguished families asked the cops, who then called reporters to demand how those pesky journalists obtained non-published telephone numbers. This created a disaster for James Rapp, and there was no recovery.

Once law enforcement made the connection between James Rapp in JonBenet's case and the Columbine Massacre,

Prostitution of Justice

the belittled Boulder Police Department could make a positive headline for themselves and the Ramseys. Several Colorado law enforcement agencies and the CBI now knew they must target information brokers as retribution for their interference in both the Ramsey and Columbine investigations.

Since December 26, 1996, the Ramseys had escaped the grasp of the Boulder Police Department but not the press. All those muckrakers stationed in Boulder had begun to run out of muck. Now, a year and a half after their invasion of Colorado to report on JonBenét, not much flesh remained on the bones of that story. Fortune presented James Rapp to the press. It was, after all, better to snare a small, soiled fish on the fringe of the Ramsey case than to lose a catch altogether for the weekly fish fry their editors demanded on deadline.

Columbine also offered law enforcement an opportunity that left them salivating. By going after Rapp, they might have a chance to net a big fish, a Great White Whale, to the struggling Ahabs of Boulder P.D., a *Globe* editor, Craig Lewis. They had long wanted to shut Lewis up, and for most persons arrested, outside of a character like J.C. Colfax, a stint in jail usually quieted the recalcitrant. With Lewis silenced, the most efficient and imaginative investigator in the JonBenet Ramsey case could no longer expose the underbelly of bureaucratic errors nor interfere with "their" investigation. The Boulder P.D. could work without Lewis leaking their guesses, conclusions, and failures. District Attorneys throughout the Denver Metropolitan area who had combined into a task force to help Alex Hunter could stop looking like losers as the case had festered absent the arrest of a murder suspect. The Ramseys' law firm of Haddon, Morgan, and Foreman had a fall guy for all that negative publicity about their clients.

The CBI worked as the police authority for the Jefferson County Grand Jury in conjunction with the Jefferson County District Attorney's Office. Dennis Hall, frail-looking but competent Assistant D.A., supervised the grand jury and presented the case against James Rapp. Agents from the CBI believed they had good reason to pursue Rapp. When Jane Cracraft's friend and former partner, Agent Brown of the CBI, came knocking, looking for someone to put the "sting" on James Rapp, private investigator Cracraft performed the service. She purchased $460 worth of information on one of Brown's fellow CBI employees, tape-recorded her conversations with Rapp, and turned over the evidence to Agent Brown. From there, the information from "the sting" went to Deputy D.A. Dennis Hall.

The CBI would make a collar on the information broker but made no progress in collaring Craig Lewis. Editors at the *Globe* bought information from private investigators, some of whom bought their information from James Rapp. The wily Lewis wasn't one of them. He had another information broker, vastly superior in information quality and professional conduct than James Rapp. Lewis' source took a more sophisticated approach. He did not advertise. He had developed sources in several sensitive areas of law enforcement, he worked under an alias (no one knew his real name), and he took care to avoid the attention that Rapp desired and attracted.

The Columbine disaster occurred in Littleton, Colorado, in suburban Jefferson County, which was under the jurisdiction of District Attorney Dave Thomas. Rapp had also located his office in Jefferson County. By going after Rapp and the press for their part in "victimizing" the Columbine victims, Thomas and the police could shed some public dissatisfaction for the way the Jefferson County Sheriff's Office had mishandled the Columbine Massacre. Thomas produced press releases of his investigation decrying James Rapp, Regana Rapp, his wife, and his companies. He directed Dennis Hall to use the grand jury to file indictments.

D.A. Thomas put Rapp out of business, but the real prizes, Craig Lewis and his information broker, slipped the noose.

The Ramseys had not blundered into retaining Hal Haddon. The Ramseys' business attorney knew and initially recommended Bryan Morgan of Haddon, Morgan, and Foreman. Morgan resided in Boulder. All the partners had cut their teeth in criminal defense through the Colorado Public Defenders' Office when it was first established in 1970. Haddon worked as the Chief Trial Deputy with his office in Jefferson County.

Prostitution of Justice

The policy of grand jury secrecy, which became one of Haddon's trademarks, kept all testimony in the hands of the Jefferson County prosecutor, Dennis Hall, and his boss, District Attorney Thomas. Best of all, the grand jury investigation into James Rapp turned the spotlight off JonBenet for a few days. The press had already stampeded from Boulder to Jefferson County to cover the Columbine Massacre.

Grand jury prosecutor Hall pursued the Rapps and their information-brokering businesses with all the power of the District Attorney's office. He spoke at the indictment of James and Regana Rapp about how terribly they had acted, falsely representing themselves and receiving money for tricking information from the grief-stricken and unknowing parents.[59] Of course, capturing information from traumatized victims and suspects isn't altogether rare or discouraged in police work. The indictment of these information brokers suggested that Thomas' office sought the felony charges to heal a community wounded by Columbine.

Dennis Hall offered Regana Rapp leniency in exchange for her testimony against her husband. She received a deferred judgment on her felony racketeering charges. The punishment for her "crimes," given for her testimony against her husband, amounted to only fifty hours of community service for dismissal of all charges two years after completing successful probation. Regana Rapp also divorced James Rapp in 1999.

Prostitution of Justice

James Rapp, the "mastermind" and most wicked of the husband-and-wife team of information brokers, received seventy-five days in jail and four years of probation. The plea agreement also required that he not engage in the private investigations business while on probation. Rapp also had to perform 200 hours of community service. He claimed he got religion from his new brush with the law and conviction. He also claimed that after his sentencing, he would devote his life to Jesus. Rapp's light sentence, given his prior conviction record, resulted from his cooperation with authorities and the fact that his most serious crime committed was lying, a crime of difficult prosecution. Perjury, lying under oath, is a crime; simply lying isn't. Hall's conscience did not shudder at the difference between the free market purchase of information derived from conning the unaware by James Rapp, who had been unmasked, and other more professional information brokers without the error-prone results.

Craig Lewis had enraged Hal Haddon by attempting to purchase a copy of the infamous ransom note from Ramsey's handwriting expert, Donald Vacca. Haddon and other lawyers from his firm who were working for the Ramseys sent a letter to D.A. Dave Thomas. They demanded the prosecution of both Lewis and his lawyer for having approached Vacca when Lewis offered $30,000 for a copy of the ransom note. Thomas didn't have the evidence to convict Lewis, as the elderly Vacca and his wife could not identify the *Globe* editor from a photo lineup.

Prostitution of Justice

In addition, Lewis's lawyer, the author, claimed attorney-client privilege in refusing to name Lewis. Nevertheless, as the Rapp investigation proceeded, D.A. Thomas and Hall thought they'd caught the scent of Lewis's blood, but the CBI, trying as they did to conquer facts with suppositions, couldn't link Craig Lewis to James Rapp's operations.

Reporters may claim information brokers as protected sources, and it is a messy legal process to pierce the shield laws that protect journalists from exposing a source. Only if the cops can find the information broker and pinpoint the access to the information can they bust them. And, although a journalist's shield law does offer some protection for a reporter, the information broker has none. A renowned information broker, Al Schweitzer[60,] had supplied illegally gathered information to ABC News. He had numerous other clients within other traditional news outlets. None of the reporters who used his information went to jail; Schweitzer did. Now, Craig Lewis, who had been wreaking havoc with the reputations of police and prosecutors, had come too close to important information too many times, and the political authorities who had a vested interest in preserving their reputations, regardless of an indictment of John and Patsy Ramsey or a mysterious intruder, wanted to shut Lewis up.

Prostitution of Justice

Chapter Seven: The Impresario of Pasta

Americans like the parents of JonBenet Ramsey, and their wealthy friends can count on a certain kindness, a greater gentility distributed by the criminal justice system than that experienced by the poor and working class. Take, for example, the Ramseys' friend and business partner, Jay Elowsky, who created a fortune out of pasta.

John and Patsy Ramsey frequented Elowsky's "Pasta Jay's" Italian restaurant just west of Boulder's Pearl Street Mall. John Ramsey took an interest in the restaurant and, voilà, became a business partner and advisor. Out of that relationship, Elowsky found himself in the center ring in the circus when he sheltered the Ramseys from the press as they hid from the search parties of photographers the media sent out for headline pictures.

Elowsky left Bay City, Wisconsin, in 1980 for San Clemente, California. His aunt and uncle owned a restaurant there, and that connection provided young Jay with work. He washed dishes and waited tables while putting in time learning how to cook, watching his relatives turn pasta into money. Still, Elowsky thought he needed more and left the family's Italian restaurant for some education at the University of Colorado in Boulder.

Academics didn't stick to Elowsky the way serving pasta had. In 1982, he returned to sunny California for an apprenticeship in the culinary arts with his aunt and uncle, where he learned both the back end and the front end of restaurant management over the next six years. Whatever didn't appeal to Jay Elowsky from book learning at CU, he made up for mastering the family recipes, those preparations brought from Europe; ingredients measured and mixed for the tables of royalty to satisfy hunger, enjoy wines, and bring people together in celebration.

As a young man with a good mind, a good family, and a work ethic, Elowsky set his course back to Boulder to open his own Italian restaurant, Pasta Jay's. His mother, Jean, and his father, Lowell, lived in Bay City, Wisconsin, and held a Federal Firearms License (FFL), which permits the sale of guns to the public. Lowell passed on his appreciation of firearms to Jay, and both parents lent their entrepreneurial son a hand with finances to start his new restaurant. Like any young businessman, Jay Elowsky struggled with taxes and payroll, rent, and food costs. Still, he did well, and then he did better when he met the man with the golden touch.

John and Patsy Ramsey loved to dine out. Boulder offered many fine restaurants, but none offered the recipes of Pasta Jay's served by beautiful young women, many of them coeds at CU, along with the reasonable prices not common in vibrant downtown Boulder. John and Patsy came to dine frequently, bringing family and entertaining friends. One friend who joined them was Mike Bynum, John's business attorney. Later, Bynum would advise John Ramsey to retain Bryan Morgan of Haddon, Morgan, and Foreman when Boulder P.D. became curious about the discovery of JonBenet's corpse in the wine cellar.

Long before JonBenet's death, John Ramsey came to recognize a business opportunity in Pasta Jay's. He formed a business relationship with Elowsky and attorney Mike Bynum to make his investment. Patsy added her design skills for changes to the restaurant's decor as John brought his considerable business acumen to the investment. Pasta Jay's profits grew, and with that growth, the business expanded with the opening of a second location in Moab, Utah.

Elowsky said his religious faith grew when he came to Boulder.[61] He met former University of Colorado football coach Bill McCartney, who gave up million-dollar contracts coaching the University of Colorado's football team to practice a higher level of Christianity and lead the Promise Keepers organization, a Christian faith group that focused on instilling religious principles in men. With JonBenet's death and fingers being pointed at the parents, Elowsky brought his Christian devotion to defend his friends and business interests.

Prostitution of Justice

Since John, Patsy, and Burke had returned to Boulder from JonBenet's funeral in Atlanta, they could not return to their 15th Street mansion. The emotional and personal catastrophe haunted the family. Equally haunting was the presence of platoons of highly paid manhunters. Private eyes combed public records, information brokers spewed gags on the unsuspecting, and television satellite trucks trolled the streets of Boulder, hunting for any shot of the Ramseys that would make the 5:00 news. Eventually, the roving bands of reporters and satellite trucks homed in on Elowsky's home, believing that the Ramseys might be hiding out in their business partner's house. The gaggle of camera mongers concluded they had found paydirt and, oblivious to the concepts of private property or privacy, they began snapping photographs through open windows, making everyone inside feel like bare skin in a mosquito swamp. On February 10, 1997, Elowsky made the unfortunate decision to scratch that itch.

Warren Schmelzer and Ira Haimann worked for Specialized Engineering. Their office building sat right behind the Elowsky home. As they sat in Warren Schmelzer's car, they could have passed as reporters or private investigators, so Pasta Jay approached them with a baseball bat. He started at the passenger side, where Ira Haimann sat, and threatened him. "Get the fuck out of here!" Elowsky shouted.

Moments earlier, Lee Frank, a freelance reporter, had called 911. He had seen Elowsky pull his BMW into the parking

Prostitution of Justice

lot of Specialized Engineering in North Boulder and frighten off a television reporter and his cameraman with that trusty aluminum baseball bat. Now, to Elowsky's misfortune, he had mistaken the two engineers for reporters.

With his baseball bat, a .40 caliber Sig Sauer handgun, and language he would never use at a Promise Keepers meeting, Pasta Jay would bring himself under the big top, center ring, in the JonBenet Ramsey Murder Pageant. The press reported how Elowsky circled Schmelzer's car, holding the bat like a caveman. When Elowsky returned to his tan-colored BMW, Schmelzer made a break for the office building and made a second call to 911. Meanwhile, back in the parking lot, Haimann faced off with Elowsky by picking up a chunk of steel pipe he found nearby. Now that both men had armed themselves with clubs and the playing field leveled, Elowsky pulled his gun. About that time, the Boulder cops arrived. They handcuffed Elowsky and seated him in a squad car.

The cops had another collar in the JonBenet Ramsey case, and luckily no one was murdered. Unlike J.T. Colfax, Elowsky had money, lawyers, and access to a kinder, gentler criminal justice system denied to the poor. Courteous and professional police officers booked and released him. True, Elowsky didn't have the attraction of a murder suspect, but every arrest let the citizens of Boulder know that the cops were on the job, even if JonBenet's killer still lurked about with pen, paper, cords for binding, and paint brushes to tighten a garrote.

All the media could gorge itself on the new arrest and give Elowsky the unwanted publicity of his display of rage that cast a shadow on the Ramseys' "We're Christians" defense.

Back at Jay Elowsky's house, Patsy had been suffering emotionally, though sedated and crying,[62] when her host, on her behalf, went postal in the parking lot next door. The Boulder Police Department knew she was there and found a legal opportunity to interview her. Neither of JonBenet's parents had consented to police interviews, on the advice of counsel, these two weeks after JonBenet's murder. Now, though, Boulder P.D. could reasonably request a statement from her regarding Elowsky's outburst. Patrick Burke, Haddon, Morgan, and Foreman's highly competent Boulder colleague for Patsy, arranged for a police interview at the office of the assistant district attorney, Pete Hofstrom, who, conveniently, had a decades-long friendship with Bryan Morgan. The Ramseys would not consent to an interview at the Boulder P.D.

Patsy showed up for the interview several weeks now after the murder, obviously "medicated."[63] She said she felt imprisoned by the media camped outside Elowsky's house. She cried. She complained of the terrible pressure. At one point, she sobbed that somebody had broken into her house and had killed her little girl. Her lawyer, Patrick Burke, stood up and stared hard into her eyes until she grew silent, and the interview ended.[64]

Prostitution of Justice

Meanwhile, Boulder P.D. had arrested Elowsky, charged him with felony menacing and unlawful carrying of a concealed weapon, and then booked him into jail before releasing him on a $2,500 bond. He had chosen to threaten several innocent parties with both a baseball bat and a handgun. Now, he hired John Stavely, a lawyer in Bynum's law firm. Elowsky replaced Brett Sawyer, the private investigator who had located the autopsy photographs, as the flavor of the day.

Threatening a person with a baseball bat and then pulling a gun on that victim who tried to defend himself would seem a more serious offense than either Sawyer's or Smith's commerce in autopsy photographs. And it was. Nevertheless, Pasta Jay, John Ramsey's business partner, would walk away with an expensive slap on the wrist once his financial juice sloshed through the justice system.

Alex Hunter's D.A.'s office charged Pasta Jay Elowsky with felony menacing because he had chosen to up the ante with a Sig Sauer handgun. Of course, a baseball bat can also be described as a deadly weapon, but Boulder, a liberal bastion, thoroughly disapproves of guns in the hands of angry citizens. Given Elowsky's clean criminal history and resources, he pleaded guilty to the felony, and under the plea agreement, he faced no trial or jury. He also had the opportunity to seal his criminal record by successfully completing one year of probation. He would have to spend a couple of weekends in jail, pay some fines, and perform community service in addition to

Prostitution of Justice

refraining from alcohol for a year. The police did keep his cool Sig Sauer .40 caliber handgun.

The conduct of buying and selling information had brought serious repercussions into the lives of Brett Sawyer, Larry Smith, James Rapp, and the other bit players in the pageant of prosecuting the small fries and bit players. Associating himself with the JonBenet murder took years of J.T. Colfax's life. Bret Sawyer lost his livelihood and had to take his family "underground" to escape the press. All had lawyers. The poor defendants served more time. All paid fines. None went to trial. Their decisions, driven first by greed and then justified as trying to help solve the mystery of JonBenet's death, turned them into outcasts and a lifetime of personal, professional, and financial damages.

Brett Sawyer hoped to help solve what he called a "sex" crime with the photographs Larry Smith sold to him. J.T. Colfax trespassed on the abandoned Ramsey property and failed to set it on fire. Jay Elowsky went ballistic, trying to protect John and Patsy Ramsey from the press. Linda Hoffman-Pugh needed to pay some rent, but she also provided Boulder P.D. with useful information about the undercurrent of Patsy's frustration with JonBenet's bedwetting and soiling. All of them confessed their actions. J.T. served over two-and-a-half years in jail. All of them except Hoffman-Pugh surrendered to Boulder P.D. for the administration of all the justice they would receive, depending

Prostitution of Justice

on their social standing and wealth. Each got what justice could be bought or supplied at government expense.

Elowsky, a defendant from the monied class, plea-bargained the felony menacing to a misdemeanor, and Hunter's office reduced the concealed weapon penalty. He served two weekends in jail on a work crew and took court-ordered anger management counseling classes. He forfeited his handgun, paid $138 in fines, and served unsupervised probation for one year. In contrast to "justice," had Elowsky pled straight up to felony menacing, he would have lost his liquor license. He did not lose his business as Sawyer did, or lose his job as did Larry Smith, nor sacrifice years of freedom as did J.T. Colfax. His money and connection to the "correct" establishment class made a difference.

To refute accusations that Ramseys' friend, Elowsky, received favored treatment, Hunter's office produced the then-most recent (1996) crime statistics. Out of 151 felony menacing cases, his office had plea-bargained to the lesser charge of misdemeanor menacing. The *Boulder Daily Camera* editorialized that Elowsky's case journeyed through the court system without a taint of favoritism. The local Boulder news outlet accused the global media of greed and zeal in their quest for ratings, claiming that they would forever draw the last drop of sensational blood from the murder of the child,[65] Boulder's Little Miss Christmas.

Prostitution of Justice

At his pretrial conference, Elowsky appeared calm and gracious. "Thanks," he said to the global media, which had come to cover his infamy in the JonBenet Ramsey Murder Pageant. His high-profile felony menacing had undermined the Ramseys' alibi that, as Christians, they and their close circle of friends could not commit raw acts of violence and uncontrolled rage. Elowsky's temper linked his faith friends to the specter that such outbursts can occur even in a Christian community.

During the sentencing hearing, Dennis Brech of the Mount Hope Lutheran Church said that Elowsky had become less excitable since undergoing his anger management counseling. University of Colorado Regent Jim Martin wrote a letter to the judge: "It's clear to me this February incident was a wakeup call to send his life in a different direction."

Elowsky said, "I've disgraced the Ramsey family, my family and friends, and the Boulder[66] community. I've caused a lot of people grief." Which people and whose grief? Schmelzer and Haimann, the two engineers, could have been murdered.

Now, the argument of Christian virtue required adjustment; if bloodthirsty reporters hadn't surrounded Elowsky's house and had left the grieving Ramseys alone, Elowsky would never have suffered for the menacing of two engineers. Elowsky's accusation from a felony menacing charge became one more opportunity to blame the press. The press interrupted their invisible privacy. The press had found John, Patsy, and Burke. The family moved out of Elowsky's bachelor

Prostitution of Justice

pad[67] after the publicity died down. All's well that ends well, but for Jay Elowsky, all too briefly.

On May 16, 1998, the arrest of Elowsky for driving under the influence of alcohol within his probationary period provided grounds for revoking his deal because he had violated the terms of his probation. Suddenly, he found the hot seat warming up for him again. But by the time of the pretrial conference for the alcohol offense on July 27, his probationary period had expired, as had the five-day window for a prosecutor to notify the defendant that his probation would be revoked. Oops! How did that routine notice escape the attention of the prosecution?

Bill Wise, Boulder's former first assistant district attorney and Hunter's right-hand man for twenty-eight years, explained that the paperwork regarding Elowsky's second arrest didn't reach Hunter's office until June 24, and the probation had expired before the office could act on the violation. John Stavely represented Elowsky again. He plea-bargained the more serious alcohol offense to a lesser charge of driving while impaired. The Impresario of Pasta rode off into the sunset, driver's license in hand, to continue selling Chianti with his pasta. The man with the golden touch withdrew from the pasta business. John Ramsey later suggested to police that Elowsky owned a stun gun, implying his possible responsibility for JonBenet's brutal death.

Prostitution of Justice

Prostitution of Justice

Part Three: Reasonable Doubt for a Reasonable Fee

Boulder Canyon - Boulder, Colorado

Prostitution of Justice

Prostitution of Justice

Chapter One: Taking Out Snakes

The Massasauga Rattlesnake lives in the swampy areas 60 miles outside of Flint, Michigan, near the rural town of Holly, where Harold "Hal" Haddon grew up. The rattlesnakes grew plentifully in his father's hayfields. His father worked as a farmer, as a schoolteacher, and to raise his two sons to work. Every day began with livestock to feed and care for or working the crops for their harvesting. His father found work character building in the way that World War II veterans wanted to raise hardworking, patriotic sons.

His prodigal son remembers that his father didn't do much of anything else but work. Occasionally, he could find it entertaining. Should he think his boys also needed some entertainment, as well as to please his wicked sense of humor, he steered the hay baler over nesting Massasauga rattlesnakes. The snakes came out mangled and bailed, dead or menacing for his sons to "harvest." The tractor puttered forward of the hardworking and perturbed boys from their father's mischievous sense of humor. Haddon could take some pleasure in "taking out"[68] the ubiquitous rattlesnakes on the 80-acre farm. Taking out snakes, or saving their human counterparts, would become

Prostitution of Justice

a metaphor for Hal Haddon's legal career and lifetime in politics.

Haddon remembers his mother with sympathy and her singing voice with delight and sadness. She had begun a career in acting when she fell in love, got married, and went to work on the farm. Hal was born in 1940, the first of two sons. His mother had to raise her sons on eighty acres with a five-acre vegetable garden while his father taught school. His mother held down the farm and sacrificed her acting and singing career, equally devoted to her sons but stranded in melancholia. Her singing voice intensified and relieved Hal's own sadness for her lost career. His mother's mistake, which brought him into existence, aroused his sensitivity to the concept of a mistake versus a conviction of guilt.

His mother believed she had married too young, and it cost her months, then bleeding into years, of unhappiness. The effects of an errant decision and a mistake emerge in Haddon's professional relationships with clients. No matter what mistake a person had made, how bad the judgment was, or how heinous the crime committed, anyone can make a mistake. Even if the course of their life is altered irrevocably, one wrong decision does not extinguish human value. Redemption can be found. His mother's sadness instilled in him a sympathy for fateful decisions, those that his clients regretted. Her sympathetic son could save a criminal, just as he hoped for his mother's happiness and salvation one day.

Prostitution of Justice

If not a happy childhood, Hal Haddon made it a good one. He learned from his mother's sacrifice and his father's endless work to seize life with both hands. He had grown up self-reliant with a strong back and determination. He had a lean, tall body and played baseball and basketball in his high school class of 60 students. He played well enough to captain the basketball team. His high school team even went to the Michigan State Finals and played for a division championship. He could have accepted an athletic scholarship to college. However, he describes himself as "a tall, skinny, white guy.[69]" Not yet certain of his future, he went on a senior trip, leaving Michigan for the first time in 1958. Like a puppy loose from a leash, he dove in with all his senses, knowing he would not make the mistake of choosing a short, average career in sports for the possibilities offered by the four-year academic scholarship to Albion College he had accepted.

Back on the farm, his mother also made a correction in her life once both her sons graduated from high school. She left the farm and Michigan to move to Sarasota, Florida. She joined a stage company and sang to the audience again. She would return to Michigan and her husband, now smiling each year for a couple of months, long enough for her to want to return to Florida. When she could no longer care for herself, her husband brought her back to Michigan, worked, and took responsibility for her until she died. Those years of his mother's return to the stage, living her dream no matter what the past, proved to Hal

Prostitution of Justice

Haddon the power of personal decisions, life-making or life-breaking, and most importantly, the power of redemption.

Four years of study in economics, history, and political science at Albion College did not challenge Haddon so much as seize his mind, clarifying the expanses of his intellect in competition with others. He found study and living easy in comparison to his childhood as one of his father's farmhands. He graduated at the top of his class. Upon the recommendation of Albion College faculty and recruitment by the University of Michigan, Haddon was offered a scholarship. There, he took an advanced degree in a subject of rising political urgency for study in modern-day America: the motivations and how to affect those motivations when citizens voted. In a word, polling.

The science began a few decades earlier when George Gallup predicted Thomas Dewey would win against Harry Truman in the 1948 election. Gallup blew it, predicting that Dewey would win in a blaring front-page headline in the Chicago Tribune depicting Harry Truman as the winner. The historic blunder served to establish a new industry with real "political scientists" like Hal Haddon. Since everything came easily to him, his studies in Arts and Humanities broadened his theoretical grasp in applying the hard science of math with psychology to fickle voters, what they believed, which issues pushed or pulled them, and how to swing and capture votes.

The work necessitated human interaction to gather raw data. That human information awaited inquiry as Haddon and

Prostitution of Justice

others interviewed prisoners at the Michigan State Prison, a famous depot of abandoned humanity. Rebuilt from 1927 to 1937, it was the largest prison in the world at its completion and capable of housing 5,700 souls, all of them suffering from their mistakes and needing redemption or at least examination.

Haddon witnessed firsthand the disparity in black lives denied equality. The young student worked in that prison to become absorbed in the economic and political history of his country. He began academia thinking of himself as a typical, though bright, country boy only to soon realize he didn't just stand taller than most people. He was smarter. He hadn't taken a typical tuition-sponsored entry into college. He put himself through Albion College and the University of Michigan on scholarships. Hal Haddon had walked right out of Michigan's snake-infested swamps and would never have to suffer the meritless slur of "typical."

When Hal Haddon began learning how to shape public opinion and predict political outcomes in 1962, the minimum wage in the United States was $1.25 per hour, $10.00 a day. For each "subject" Haddon contacted and interviewed, the student scholar received $20.00. Hal Haddon could earn two days' pay in a single interview. He worked hard, farming now for his future instead of alfalfa. For that future, he learned about the psychology of humans as they expressed opinions, beliefs, and values. He gained an understanding of political science both inside and outside of the classroom. He gained not only financially, much to the satisfaction of a farm boy, but also an understanding of how beliefs and related opinions could influence a person to turn out for or against an ideal. In this respect, psychological and sociological science left lab rats and dogs in their cages to study human subjects. Mazes consisted of questionnaires, and social Pavlovian responses were refined by applying scientific principles, pinpointing attitudes left and right. He had left the Massasauga Rattlesnake for a higher breed of snakes: politicians.

Elvin Remus Latty, a former graduate of the University of Michigan Law School, Class of 1930, and once the Dean of Duke University Law School beginning in 1957, learned of the rising Hal Haddon at his alma mater and recruited him again on an academic scholarship. Latty, who had taught Romance languages before entering law, worked for a few years as an associate for a New York City law firm. He worked in corporate law and explored closely held corporations versus the needs of individual and smaller entities[70] before returning to academics and teaching.

Latty's corporate work may have glazed the eyes of many lawyers, but by the 1960s, the big business structure of organizations had been reorganized, and Congress passed legislation reducing the legal and paperwork expenses for individuals and small groups to form corporations. The spreading of the corporate umbrella and its protections over small investors resulted in the remaking of a new, smaller, more agile business class. Big Business would have to compete with a strengthening middle class of entrepreneurs, the little guys.

Duke University Law School's Dean Elvin Latty placed significant importance on the "little guy" obtaining justice in a world of "Big Dog" economic power. During his tenure, he amassed the brightest scholars and students of law he could recruit in the United States. He imagined and created The World Rule of Law Center in 1962, the same year a tall, young, and talented kid from a Michigan farm accepted a scholarship to Duke University Law School.

Before his fall enrollment at Duke in 1962, Hal Haddon and some college friends took a road trip: Washington D.C., Upper Pennsylvania, across the northeastern United States all the way to Seattle, down California's Highway 101, and even Colorado on a side trip.

Hal Haddon saw the majestic Rocky Mountains as the car rolled in from the eastern plains. The snowcapped peaks struck him as if they were "pyramids."[71] The mountains of Colorado uplifted Hal Haddon as much as Hal Haddon would uplift the Democratic Party with which he had aligned himself.

On March 18, 1963, in the spring semester, while Hal Haddon powered through Duke University Law School, Clarence Earl Gideon, through his court-appointed lawyer, Abe Fortas, overturned a century of American law. The Supreme Court of the United States had crept forward to apply the Civil

Prostitution of Justice

War-era protections of the 14th Amendment to all states. By 1942, in Betts v. Brady,[72] the Supreme Court ruled that an indigent defendant didn't necessarily violate the 14th Amendment Right to Counsel. In capital cases, the death penalty raised the stakes, and courts owed a defendant fair trial representation by counsel when the government imposed the death penalty, the ultimate loss of life, liberty, and the pursuit of happiness. That left defendants to fend for themselves in battery, burglary, larceny, and lesser felonies until Mr. Gideon, using the prison library, drilled through the Constitution, and with his lead pencil, filed a brief to appeal his criminal sentence. Henry Fonda starred as Clarence Earl Gideon in his historic civil rights victory in the 1980 movie adaptation of Gideon's Trumpet.

As the top student at his school, Hal Haddon, the Editor of the Duke Law Review, had the opportunity to examine contemporary legal and philosophical directions in law, especially in a change so profound as Gideon v. Wainwright. The American Criminal Justice System must apply equality of rights in every state, and that includes legal representation by a lawyer. Society had moved a long way forward since 1868 and the passage of the 14th Amendment. Under Gideon, each state, county, city, or town must apply rights equally, including free legal representation if the accused was indigent.

Haddon's academic studies, his interviews, and his heart drove his social conscience when, on November 22, 1963, fall semester, while playing basketball, Hal Haddon lived the national nightmare, a mortal moment for all the world, when President John F. Kennedy was assassinated. The effect of that murder would reverberate through the rest of Haddon's professional and private life.

Hal Haddon had entered Albion College at seventeen and may never have graduated from more than high school without the brains for scholarships and his own grit. He knew self-sufficiency and was raised by his father's hard work and from within the shroud of his mother's melancholia. Kennedy's assassination ignited him along with the rest of the nation. For "better or worse,"[73] Haddon entered into lifelong political activism as a Democrat rooted in the Civil Rights Movement. Attending Duke in Durham, North Carolina, he applied his work ethic and grad school scientific methods of analyzing public opinion into self-taught basic training in marches, sit-ins at lunch counters, and demonstrations against the KKK. Duke University graduated Hal Haddon in 1966, and, of course, he graduated number one in his class.

Chapter Two: Mountains Like Pyramids

The young Hal Haddon, newly minted lawyer, knew where he wanted to live and returned to Colorado. He had also met his wife, Beverly, the year before, and together they journeyed to the Centennial State. Davis, Graham & Stubbs, a top-drawer Denver law firm founded in 1915, hired the freshly minted, insanely intelligent Hal Haddon.

The new associate attorney could have gone anywhere, but the confident young lawyer made his own decisions. He only regretted not accepting a Rhodes Scholarship because of a sense of inadequacy, that he hadn't grown up with enough sophistication for Oxford.[74] Instead, he made his move to scenic Colorado. He arrived before public defender offices had opened nationwide to handle the poor under the demands of Gideon v. Wainwright. In those developing years between Gideon in 1963 and 1969, when Colorado created the nation's first Colorado Public Defenders Office, Hal Haddon worked predominantly in business law and bankruptcy. Until public defender offices could be opened and staffed nationwide, courts assigned cases to the local bar, where Haddon got a taste of criminal defense.

Court-appointed counsel would shrug, perhaps groan, as the court removed them from their lucrative practice to defend the "presumed innocent." The imposed-upon lawyer may have practiced brilliantly in property or water law. Unfortunately, the

Prostitution of Justice

Gideon ruling did not require that a specialist in criminal defense and trial work be drafted for clients on the criminal docket. Any lawyer from any legal field would do, even if that meant doing poorly.

Hal Haddon was a member of the bar who had established relationships in his bankruptcy practice. However, about the time of Gideon, the Denver Board of Education came under national scrutiny for its segregated public schools. The practice of racial discrimination fit exactly into the political and personal belief system that disgusted Hal Haddon, and he would not let stand the evils he had witnessed and had been trained to fight against before, during, and now after law school. He speaks of Denver's landmark school desegregation case with satisfaction following his work in the years of demonstrations, controversy, and a "sensational trial"[75] that would order Denver Public Schools to end racial discrimination district-wide.

With that decision, the next generation of Denver citizens would learn about the equality of races by being bussed throughout the Denver Public Schools according to a standard of racial quotas. Many Denver families sold their homes and moved to the suburbs in a "white flight" from Denver's public schools, bussing, and racial desegregation. The temperature of the public grew white-hot as racist vigilantes set fire to Denver school buses, damaging or destroying a third of the fleet.

Haddon staked out much of his involvement in the Democrat party as he volunteered to work on the ground in the

Prostitution of Justice

Denver Civil Rights Movement. He brought with him a farmer's work ethic, knowing a good crop requires a lot of spade and shovel work. He set about to garner attention to move issues in or out of minds of voters, to identify votes precinct by precinct, and to find and foster the activists to lead in a massive urban vote farm.

Before walking the precincts, the literature was prepared and printed with the message scientifically formulated to draw supporters to cast their ballots. His wife, Beverly, enjoyed social interactions in politics within those campaigns. The couple met other activists privately, at caucuses and party conventions, or while walking precincts, all the while establishing relationships inside the political hierarchy of the Democrat Party. Those connections helped to establish Hal Haddon's political power from Denver to throughout Colorado and beyond, all the way to the nation's capital in Washington, D.C.

Future Senator Gary Hart, a graduate of Yale Law School, had also arrived in Colorado in 1965 as a solicitor for the United States Department of Interior. By 1968, Hart left public service to practice law at Davis, Graham & Stubbs. There, he and Hal Haddon could practice law in a camaraderie of shared political beliefs. Civil Rights via political activism pushed all the Democrat Party after the April 4, 1968, assassination of Martin Luther King. In that violent year, Hal Haddon focused his mind and his ambition on the political lift needed for Robert F. Kennedy's campaign. Haddon worked on the ground in Colorado, performing the duties of an advance man, arranging for accommodations and seating. Security was also Haddon's responsibility.

The Washington insider from Yale Divinity School, Gary Hart, managed Kennedy's national campaign. June 6, 1968, Kennedy rose to the top of the competition, a locomotive of momentum, after winning the California Democratic Primary Election. The campaign catastrophically derailed that night when RFK was assassinated in a Los Angeles hotel kitchen. That murder of the front-runner helped spark the riots that broke out at the 1968 Democratic National Convention in Chicago.

The calamitous death of Robert Kennedy propelled the already surging fury of an American generation that did not want to fight the Vietnam War. Young revolutionaries showed up in Chicago to support Eugene McCarthy, a Minnesota Senator. McCarthy had entered the primaries as an antiwar Democrat before Lyndon Johnson surprisingly bowed out and would not seek re-election. The peace candidate followers of McCarthy were disappointed in the courtly world of genteel political conventions and nominations.

Galvanized firebrands of the far left applied the methods used to dislodge Czars, Kaisers, and Emperors of the early 20th Century. Young men facing the draft could fight on Chicago's streets or in Vietnam, and if drafted, both. The Socialists for a

Prostitution of Justice

Democratic Society (SDS) led the riots against the Vietnam War, which were televised in parallel with endless images of helpless almond-eyed children and the human slaughter in rice paddies halfway around the world. Fire, police clubs, and bloodletting on Chicago streets were broadcast worldwide in a real political crisis in the United States.

Richard Nixon won the White House in 1968, and the Vietnam War continued. Hal Haddon immersed himself back at work with Denver's 17th Ave. lawyers at Davis, Graham & Stubbs in the American Bank Building. Back in Colorado, in response to the mandates of Gideon v. Wainwright, the Centennial State created its Public Defenders Office in 1969. The new experiment in equal justice needed trial lawyers and found a Southwestern Colorado Cowboy to head up the office.

Rollie Rogers was born in Southwestern Colorado in the town of Alamosa in rural Bent County, where he hunted for Indian artifacts and arrowheads in his youth. His family pioneered their way to the Southwest from Illinois. He grew up respecting Native Americans, particularly the Cheyenne People, so much so that he designed a Cheyenne symbol in red, white, and blue that he copied for his belt buckle, bolo tie, and accessories to embrace his flamboyant personality.

Rogers grew up in a small town with friendly, Western hospitality, speaking in the lingo of the West, often gulping whiskey, and he loved animals. He enlisted and served in the U.S. Army during World War II, and he survived through its duration.[76] In cowboy boots and wearing a business suit, he addressed acquaintances and strangers as "Partner" with a smile under his cowboy hat. He also chewed tobacco, often missed the spittoon, and had tried many death penalty cases. Like Hal Haddon, he thought a government that would kill its own citizens was abhorrent. His hopes for legislation banning the ultimate penalty in Colorado went down in flames when the Statehouse kept the penalty on the books.

On the elevator riding to the 14th floor of the American Bank Building, Haddon, the civil rights worker, political scientist, and corporate lawyer, met Rogers, the pure criminal defense trial lawyer who liked fees but fought for justice. Haddon had tried a few criminal defense cases for indigent clients while working for Davis, Graham & Stubbs before Gideon v. Wainwright forced the creation of the Colorado Public Defenders Office in 1969.

Democrat Governor Dick Lamm appointed the spitting, brassy, and irresistible Rollie Rogers as Colorado's first State Public Defender. Not only could he persuade a jury, but Rogers also persuaded Hal Haddon to leave his profitable employment at Davis, Graham & Stubbs for public service, representing the poor in Jefferson County, one of the first three P.D. offices in Colorado. The first capitol in Colorado was located in Colorado City, located in Jefferson County in 1861, which had matured into a large suburban county west of Denver. There, prosecutors would meet a new generation of legal firebrands on a mission of equal justice, fighting the death penalty, and redesigning the criminal justice system. The work promised many new court dockets to make room for all the lawyers and trials formerly unavailable to the poor, still victimized, but now with lawyers.

Hal Haddon had made it out of the Michigan swamps and their Massasauga Rattlesnakes to Colorado in July 1965 at 25 years of age. He took the bar exam and got his license, and now, he drives a courtroom hay baler and mangles law snakes with sloppy police work or witnesses with an agenda. Assistant D.A.s and former D.A.s who had made it onto the bench as judges had sent citizens to bulging prisons with little opposition beyond a political agenda since Colorado Statehood in 1876. The staffs in District Attorney's Offices would need to expand.

Hal Haddon began making headlines winning trials and death penalty cases in Jefferson County while Rollie Rogers did likewise in Denver. Once, they brought in not-guilty verdicts for murder charges on the same day: Haddon winning in Jefferson County and Rogers in Denver. The press loved the drama created in the courtroom. Hal Haddon shunned flashbulbs, interviews, and the press he could not control. He likely learned from his graduate work at the University of Michigan that a single slip could swamp an agenda.

Rollie Rogers, on the other hand, with brash Southwestern style, cowboy boots, hats, and bolo ties, brought character and color, and no lack of "true grit." The press did not appeal to Haddon except in its power. However, both Rogers and Haddon thrived on acquittals. Until a person experiences a criminal trial from the defendant's table, the release from teeth-grinding jeopardy and the first new breath of freedom returns hope and release in a flash from the specter of bondage that engulfs everyone on the defense team. It's an endorphin rush no drug can match.

To ride that high, everyone got on board: lawyers, secretaries, and especially the investigators, a team of them unlike the black-and-white television series Perry Mason with only private eye, Paul Drake. The lawyers still starred in the show. Unlike the single investigator Paul Drake, tall, suave, and intelligent, arriving to save the day with a startling new fact, Rollie Rogers and Hal Haddon would still star in the courtroom, but their private investigators uncovered the facts that would startle juries and save real-life clients from real death penalties.

Wally Barrett, a jolly red-headed man of Irish descent, worked as a bartender across from the Capitol Building on Colfax Ave. at the upscale Quorum Restaurant in 1970. No one could light a cigarette at Wally's bar before the big-hearted bartender had a lighter at the tip of the cigarette, always flashing his big-hearted smile. A cowboy from the Western Slope with a degree in Drama, Wally could assume any character on the stage to find his hook, his human connection of trust, which filled him with secrets, one cocktail at a time.

Rogers, a regular at the bar, hired Barrett into his office

Prostitution of Justice

to train him as a private investigator in the Denver Office. Hal Haddon came across a stout, intense, black-haired investigator in Jefferson County, David Williams. These two, and others, would read the discovery, find the witnesses, study the evidence, conduct the interviews the cops had missed, and serve the subpoenas on the front lines, then testify. These trailblazers began to realize their passion for civil rights and equality of justice, not in anonymous demonstrations but in the courtrooms where facts can confirm or deny innocence and restore freedom.

Colorado's Public Defenders offices first opened in Denver and Jefferson County, immediately west of Denver, on January 1, 1970. Hal Haddon took command in Jefferson County, where he and his staff handled two to three hundred cases at a time. There were trials before juries, and all of Hal Haddon's intellect and education came to bear. He understood humans from hundreds, perhaps thousands, of individual interviews and the analysis of the responses into distinct demographics. He could pick a jury starting with the questionnaire, and from there, he began to persuade them how to vote not guilty.

Haddon commanded the courtroom, usually the tallest man in the room, astonishingly well prepared and beaming with sheer brilliance. Rogers, Haddon, and the new, fire-breathing criminal defense lawyers fresh from the civil rights movement carried their beliefs in equality to juries. They would meet their future partners for their later move into private practice,

Prostitution of Justice

Bryan Morgan and Lee Foreman, through their association in public defense. These new warriors of social justice carried the loss of not just John F. Kennedy but Martin Luther King and Bobby Kennedy in their hearts. From their generation of protest, they brought their ideas and passion into the courtroom. They worked as a team: lawyers, investigators, secretaries, and paralegals all focused on a new calling in public service, defending the people who had never experienced representation by a lawyer or trusted in the right to an attorney guaranteed in the Constitution. Now, the accused met someone who knew what the words in the law meant and could explain the mysteries outside of a man in a black robe who likely would use those words to put him in prison or kill him. All races had access to courts with rights acknowledged and ignored since the Civil War.

Like General Grant, Rollie Rogers earned a reputation for winning and his appreciation for whiskey. His work near the Capitol placed him conveniently across Colfax Avenue from the Quorum, a favorite watering hole of politicos. Rogers could relax at the bar and conduct his unofficial business first class. Wally Barrett and Rogers related to each other. They both drank a lot and grew up far from Denver on the Western Slope. The red-headed cowboy could also sing and play the piano in addition to his degree in Drama. He could assume any character on the stage, or from the street, to find his hook, a human

Prostitution of Justice

connection that would give way to a person's trust, filling him with secrets, one cocktail at a time. Barrett made anyone his audience with a joke or making a face, a dance, a pose. With a gigantic heart, he loved the memory of his mother with the reverence of an Irish son. He lived like a misplaced priest with his open, charitable heart.

God also gifted him with a dramatist's deep voice that would soothe, smooth, and comfort a witness to gain uncanny trust from untrustworthy persons as they surprised themselves by revealing confidences, letting go of words meant to be kept secret even while they lied, denied, or confessed. He could also go round for round of drinks with Rollie Rogers or anyone else and hold their secrets as well as he could hold his whiskey.

Denver's 17th St. Davis, Graham & Stubbs lost 30-year-old Hal Haddon to Rollie Rogers and public service. The Quorum had to replace Wally Barrett for Rollie Rogers to introduce him to private investigation. Around the same time in 1971, Hal Haddon found a stout, intense, black-haired investigator in the Jefferson County P.D. office, David Williams. That relationship would last a lifetime along with many of the young Turks who joined Haddon's future: law firm partners Bryan Morgan and Lee Foreman, a future 10th U.S. District Judge, Michael Kane, and Joe Quinn who went on to assume the position of the Chief Justice of the Colorado Supreme Court. J.D. McFarland was elected the Colorado Attorney General and later entered the state legislature. Rollie

Prostitution of Justice

Rogers had raised a crop of drop-dead and damned good trial lawyers. Facts won cases, and Haddon had command of his facts at the top of the legal team as a premier trial lawyer. If the lawyer's facts raised enough reasonable doubt, the team won.

When Haddon recalls clients[77] he saved from the executioner, he acknowledges their human mistakes and decisions ending in a human death. He believes in an act of redemption because another life, the accused, was not taken by the state to avenge the dead. A guiding principle of his representation began in trying to understand why this happened to his client. He found the human inside with a study in excruciating detail of facts. He remained friends with many clients he led through their trial of fire. Some refer to him as the familial "Uncle." He had established himself as one of the best trial lawyers in Colorado, and the nation took notice of his skills in fighting the Nixon Administration's Drug War.

Colorado's Governor, Dick Lamm, next called on Hal Haddon. This time, Haddon would not wear out district attorneys before juries; he would investigate, wiretap, and arrest drug traffickers, wearing out organized crime. Governor Lamm asked him to switch sides from public defender to grand jury prosecutor in charge of the Colorado Organized Crime Strike Force. Since the United States had grown a drug problem, the appropriate political response from Washington was to address the social blight with a drug war and, by association, organized crime. Haddon's assumption of power in the Colorado legal system, combined with unparalleled knowledge of grand jury proceedings and personal relationships with D.A.s, Sheriff's officers, and political muckety-mucks throughout the state would not only shape his future law practice but also shape legislators and lawmakers throughout Colorado and the United States.

Chapter Three: Yee Olde Grand Jury

In Denver, Colorado, at the intersections of Interstate 70, East and West, and Interstate 25, North and South, narcotics traffic met at a national crossroads. With his new position as a Special Prosecutor, Hal Haddon had the opportunity to travel.

Aspen, Vail, and the Summit County Ski Areas lay along the I-70 corridor through the Rocky Mountains. Telluride, Purgatory, and Wolf Creek to the south invited those who could afford the sport; the lifestyle and the drugs that made the adventure more expensive beckoned as Hal Haddon's forces investigated and indicted the dealers. He could turn small-time users into snitches to reel in bigger and bigger fish, gaining recognition from his rare experience inside the ironworks of government, his real courtroom knowledge, and now, raw political power. Elected District Attorneys, their Assistant D.A.s, Sheriffs, down to the local town cop either worked at his disposal or, if naughty and snared, were prosecuted. His appointment from the Democrat Party presented him with more power as a special grand jury prosecutor than most people could ever know or understand in a lifetime.

That appointment marked a dichotomy in Haddon's career. The civil rights movement had drawn him to the defendant's table; now, he stood before the bench as a prosecutor, using the same fact-driven investigations, but now he had eliminated the guesswork of the defense. He held the power of the grand jury, the subpoena, and its secret operations. He offered shorter terms of imprisonment for the fish caught in his net if they chose not only to confess but testify against their greedy, violent, and even homicidally prone associates.

The grand jury precedes the United States Constitution all the way back to Merry Old England until 1933, when it ceased to function and was abolished in England in 1948.[78] The English Grand Jury had changed from a secretly gathered group of citizens. They once acted as neighborhood informants who would meet secretly to identify culprits in their community and forward those indicted to the King's judges for a trial. For centuries, a court usher employed by the King would guide the grand juries through the witnesses and evidence, and after centuries of use, indictments became perfunctory. Only in rare cases would juror upstarts to the King's power refuse a true bill to the prosecutor to become a "runaway" grand jury.

This worked well as Europe sought enlightenment after the Dark Ages, driving their oxcarts through history before Western Civilization would employ constables, marshals, police officers, sheriffs, and lawyers to assume responsibility for public safety. As time moved on, much of it still by oxcart, into the 20th century, England had lost the United States, faced Napoleon at Waterloo, colonized much of the rest of the world, and fought endless wars. England realized the perfunctory indictments of secret grand juries made at the direction of government prosecutors had outlived their usefulness, except in London and the County of Middlesex, where treason or crimes committed under the jurisdiction of the Official Secrets Act survived. Even those were abolished in England in 1948.

At the time of the American Revolution, citizens quite clearly wanted nothing of England's tyrannical government and enshrined the grand jury in the Fifth Amendment to the Constitution: "No person shall be held to answer for a capital or otherwise infamous crime unless on presentment or indictment of a Grand Jury . . ." That bedrock protection, along with the rights against self-incrimination, denial of life, liberty, and property without due process, has survived a thousand years since its roots in England. However, the clandestine power of secrecy, denial of a lawyer to witnesses or the accused, and forced testimony against oneself under penalty of imprisonment that can result, even in death, survives as well.

Despite the landmark decision in Gideon v. Wainwright, a grand jury carries all the clout of English Monarchs in the United States of America, and only on the rarest occasions are the identities of citizens or witnesses, or the perfunctory manner of indictments revealed to the public. To violate the citizen oath of grand jury secrecy promises the rebellious citizen severe and certain redress, contempt of court, and loss of liberty to a cell.

Grand Juries assemble in counties, cities, and U.S. District Courthouses. A juggernaut of case law and rules paves

Prostitution of Justice

the lanes of secret criminal investigations and usually "justice." The Grand Jury is the exclusive property of the government, and all the power of government gathers into the hands of District Attorneys or Special Prosecutors, of which Hal Haddon was the chosen one in Colorado to combat organized crime. He assumed his new powers with the same hard work, shrewd mind, and penetrating investigations. Now, though, Haddon had an army of law enforcement officers and an arsenal of wiretaps, subpoenas, and secrecy for "taking out snakes." Haddon never sought the limelight, and his privacy was as important as his politics. He worked almost as a phantom while a drug war general. The press could only guess what went on in Grand Jury Proceedings but covered the gaps with references to "La Cosa Nostra," the Mafia, and the glamorous mobsters in New Jersey and New York City.

Hal Haddon avoided and received little press as he consolidated his courtroom mastery at the prosecutor's table, as he had formerly from the defendants' side of the courtroom. He held the power of the state in his hands all the way from the top of the United States Judiciary. Robert F. Kennedy had promoted the formation of a federalized assault on organized crime.

This new Strike Force would divide the nation into sections. Special Prosecutors would lead teams of federal, state, and county prosecutors combined with state and federal law enforcement in the Organized Crime Task Force. Haddon could work with court-authorized wiretaps and search warrants.

Prostitution of Justice

David Williams worked with him to locate and interview the witnesses, and the team methodically uncovered who took bribes, who paid bribes, and who controlled the bribery and the drugs. Haddon found a little-known and almost never applied Colorado Statute, "Commercial Bribery," to effect his prosecutions.

According to Williams, "We lived inside that statute."[79]

The text of the statute bears reproduction to understand the ease with which the low-level felony could snare a suspect under broad and innocent circumstances. It has been massively revised since its abuse in charges against the author in Jefferson County, Colorado, 00 CR 2023. Yet, at the time of Haddon's Drug Strike Force, it could snare a witness or a suspect for anything from offering a cup of coffee to an undercover cop or the cop demanding $50,000 to keep a secret. The statute, as used by Hal Haddon during his work as a prosecutor, read as follows:

Colorado Revised Statutes: Commercial Bribery §18-5-401:

A person commits a class 6 felony if he solicits, accepts, or agrees to accept any benefit as consideration for knowingly violating or agreeing to violate a fidelity to which he is subject as:

(a) Agent or employee; or

(b) Trustee, guardian, or other fiduciary; or

(c) Lawyer, physician, accountant, appraiser, or other professional adviser; or

(d) Officer, director, partner, manager, or other participant in the direction of the affairs of an incorporated or unincorporated association; or arbitrator or other purportedly disinterested adjudicator or referee."[80]

That vague, wobbly statute, with its language of "any benefit," turned Colorado's Organized Criminals into a mass production line of snitches. While on his path, Haddon shined under the blue skies of Colorado, sniffing out dope, drugs, and gangsters. From Denver's I-25 and I-70 Interstate crossroads, Haddon coordinated with prosecutors nationally from within the United States Justice Department. He now exercised the extraordinary powers of prosecutors. He knew the procedures and applied them, all while absorbing the majestic power in the use of secrecy from behind the scenes. He extended his political reach throughout the counties of Colorado. He also seems to have enjoyed his work. In the decades to come, Haddon would influence revision of Grand Jury laws in Colorado to protect John and Patsy Ramsey from prosecution years after he carved his initials into the oak trees surviving in the lush, green swamp of the Washington D.C. establishment.

Hal Haddon resigned on December 31, 1973, from the Colorado Drug Task Force to work for Gary Hart's successful U.S. Senate campaign. Haddon began managing Hart's campaign on January 1, 1974. He took on Hart's campaign with

Prostitution of Justice

his distinctive work ethic and unique brilliance. Taking a page from his law practice, Haddon and his team investigated two-term incumbent Peter Dominic. They analyzed Dominic's life through the lens of every speech, every vote, and every move of the Republican who first held public office in 1961 as a U.S. House Representative from Denver. Dominic got caught in the electoral blowout ignited by the Watergate Scandal. On the night of his defeat at the fizzled watch party at the Brown Palace Hotel, a reporter asked for Dominic's comment on his impending loss. "They're full of prunes," a clearly inebriated Dominic slurred, ". . . full of prunes."

Voters scrubbed Republicans from many political offices amid the Watergate scandal and a nation exhausted by the Vietnam War. Haddon went back to scrubbing organized crime until the office simply began to wind down, or at least, had lost its luster for a man dedicated to law and who needed challenging work like banks need money. He went into private practice, bringing investigator David Williams with him in 1976. Brian Morgan from the Public Defender's Office reunited with him, and a year later, Lee Foreman would bring his P.D. experience to complete Haddon, Morgan & Foreman.

These three men had taken criminal defense to a new level. They entered law at a time when Gideon v. Wainwright mandated lawyers into the courtroom. They used teams of investigators. Haddon knew prosecution from inside and out from his work on the Organized Crime Strikeforce, and he knew

Prostitution of Justice

cops, prosecutors, and the politically connected in every corner of Colorado. All the partners of the law firm could take witnesses apart on the stand while laying out a blanket of sympathy for their accused clients. Haddon brought a suitcase full of contacts from campaign work stretching from Gary Hart to Washington, D.C. They knew they were exceptional and had exceptional hubris as they formed their slogan, "Reasonable Doubt for a Reasonable Fee," and selected a coiled rattlesnake as a symbol, a warning not necessarily limited to prosecutors.

In 1987, Haddon's good friend, Gary Hart, began a run for President of the United States. Haddon had managed Hart's two successful Senate campaigns in Colorado but declined to manage the presidential bid. They had their personal agreements and agendas, but Hal Haddon had his law firm and seemed to have been comfortable practicing law.

Gary Hart was a lawyer, but he could capture imaginations outside of the courtroom. At a small campaign stop early during the Democratic primary campaign, he stepped onto a table and took command of the room. The cameras captured a televised image of a standout candidate, an orator, and a cowboy. He gave a speech about the way politicians give speeches. No one remembers the content of the speech, but no one could forget the image of a bold, handsome Gary Hart in the mold of a statesman, not a politician.

The press played Hart that day as the Prince Valiant of the presidential race. Except for a Washington D.C.-sized, self-affirming hubris, Gary Hart may have run against George Bush for the 43rd U.S. President. Hart, unfortunately, would disappointingly recast himself in the inappropriate light of a man without strong moral character.

The word "hubris" comes from Greek. More than the generic English definition of pride, the original translation is "wanton violence arising from pride." Gary Hart had a whispered reputation as a lady's man and a womanizer. Gossip picked up on marital separations from his wife, a missing father, and troubles in his marriage. What about the extramarital rumor New York Times reporter asked.

"Go ahead, follow me. You'll be very bored," Hart said.

Who doesn't like a challenge? Hart could have been telling a cowboy to "throw down" across a poker table, but Gary Hart was no Doc Holliday. He also wasn't a pitiful, consumptive alcoholic, nor a man killer. Hart wasn't feared or hated, but he did gamble. The Miami Herald followed Hart. Reporters found him again in Florida.

The photograph that appeared in newspapers and tabloids around the world on March 3, 1987, depicted Gary Hart holding Donna Rice, a pharmaceutical sales rep and model, on his lap. She exposed tan legs under a white robe. Her arm is around Hart's shoulders, and she wears an easy smile and a dreamy look, smitten and confident. He appears less comfortable. His eyes meet the camera straight on, but his mouth is open as if in a gasp or a surprise. He is still relaxed, comfortably dressed in shorts and a white t-shirt with "Monkey Business Crew" that would highlight his wanton pride.

Gary Hart had nowhere to turn but Hal Haddon. The genius had engineered Hart's first and second U.S. Senate races. He had worked with the press to elect many Democrats. Haddon had established a Washington D.C. clientele with multinational corporations through the years with Hart. Now, Haddon's friend in the Senate needed someone he could trust. He needed someone whom Ben Bradley, Executive Editor of the Washington Post, could trust. Maybe the publisher could steer the tabloid torpedo into gossip columns, undermine it, bury it? Hart would want Hal Haddon to make the difficult call to Bradley.

How does a difficult conversation of impossible hope resolve?[81] Poorly.

Washington Post reporter Paul Taylor attended Gary Hart's press conference to address the headlines. He asked Hart, "Have you ever committed adultery?"

The table-clambering cowboy image from the campaign trail, with John Kennedy's charisma, evaporated into disgust and derision. Hart withdrew from the presidential primaries as his support collapsed in five days, on March 13, 1987. The Washington Post ran the headline: "Miami woman is linked to Hart: Candidate denies any impropriety." Hal Haddon learned

Prostitution of Justice

to despise tabloids and the press in general long before he defended John Ramsey.

Prostitution of Justice

Chapter Four: Desert Glow

Under the threat of nuclear annihilation like Hiroshima and Nagasaki, the United States built a nuclear trigger factory during the Cold War years south of Boulder along Colorado State Highway 93 called Rocky Flats. The "triggers" manufactured in the buildings of the rural plant used radioactive material in a small nuclear explosion to generate the necessary heat for the larger bomb package's devastation. By 1988, the Rocky Flats nuclear trigger factory occupied 6,655 acres of prime Colorado prairie sixteen miles northeast of Denver at the foot of the Rocky Mountains.

The Atomic Energy Commission (AEC) opened the plant in 1952 to "hoorahs" in the *Denver Post*, welcoming the invaluable defense project. It opened as a closely guarded national secret, of course, and a treasure chest of strategic annihilation should enemies of the United States become necessarily incinerated. In times of the Red Scare and McCarthyism reign in Washington, the nation and Colorado residents accepted the need for strategic defense, and the local post-Korean War economy would "boom."

The AEC had chosen a rural location on mostly untouched prairies. Dow Chemical opened the plant, which soon came under the management of Rockwell International, Inc.

Prostitution of Justice

Both the U.S. and the U.S.S.R. struggled with only a greenhorn understanding of a mankind-killing technology at the dawn of the nuclear age. Somehow, the destruction of the environment with radioactive waste was all part of developing the atomic bombs safely and trusting the government. The American free press would alert Americans if their safety were at issue. Russia didn't encounter transparency issues, and the arms race began. New suburbs and businesses in Arvada and Westminster cropped up, suburbs near Boulder, even as far north as Marshall, immediately south of Boulder. The new factory had brought the promised new jobs to the developing Denver suburbs.

On September 11, 1957, a fire broke out in Rocky Flats Building 71, used for processing plutonium. The building contained phosphorus, and dust had spread throughout it to various depths, accumulating in the hidden corners of chimneys, ducts, and vents. Phosphorus is highly flammable and prone to explode dramatically if doused with water. The employees battling the fire knew this, but the fire, which had started in a "fireproof" area, had defied the engineering estimates needed for fireproofing and proceeded to engulf the highly phosphoric plutonium air filters, thus threatening the roof, which could lead to an even greater disaster. Water overcame their better judgment, and they lugubriously applied hoses until a blue flash signaled that an atomic chain reaction had occurred and blew up the building.

Prostitution of Justice

This thwarted the firefighting efforts as the small nuclear explosion poured radioactive-laden dust particles into the night skies, offering a strong dose of airborne cancer to residents of Adams County, Denver, and points beyond as it rode the zephyrs. The explosion also left strontium 90 and cesium 135 in the soil. The presence of these elements proved that a nuclear chain reaction had occurred. In the interest of national security, officials of the Atomic Energy Commission (AEC) buried the radioactive secret.

Before and after the 1957 fire, with the production of an arsenal of nuclear triggers, plutonium waste increased. Management temporarily stored the deadly yuk in 55-gallon drums, some of which began leaking within a couple of years. Over the decades, the drums rusted and leaked, and the stockpile grew to a round number of about 4500 drums. Employees and managers became increasingly cognizant that they all participated in destroying the natural environment and may not have done so innocently.

Part of the improvised storage plan used surface pits and trenches for disposal, which became sludge ponds, literally glowing orange, streaked in hellish hues of deep blue, black, and green under which nothing survived. They rotted in radiation until leaking, leaching through the soil into the groundwater, eventually reaching suburban water taps, poisoning the population.

Prostitution of Justice

Along with open uranium oxidation ponds, Rocky Flats provided storage of nerve gas stockpiles, outlawed after World War I but kept just in case the prohibitions of the Geneva Convention would need to be defied. The secret of weapons of mass destruction, along with the secret of the 1957 fire, lasted until a second fire broke out on May 11, 1969. This fire behaved quite well in comparison to the first fire except for the public attention it drew. The public, roiled from the Vietnam War, had lost trust in the government, and pollution weighed on the minds of citizens more than the Cold War.

After the Mother's Day Fire in 1969, the secrets of Rocky Flats soon crawled from their glowing ponds into a public abomination. Property owners and the public learned for the first time of the plumes of deadly plutonium from 1957, only after the nuclear bonfire caused 12 years earlier leaked into the press as the nuclear waste spread over the prairies. Now, secrets about surface and groundwater contamination were reported, but the press was ineffective. Nothing happened to stop the pollution. Instead, Rocky Flats purchased additional acreage surrounding the plant to establish a greater defensive perimeter, or a "buffer zone" in political terms, in which it could better conceal its secrets.

The pollution went on swimmingly. Engineers studying the problem and wanting some means to continue bomb production found a possible solution. Without much testing or a forward-looking environmental examination, the engineers

Prostitution of Justice

created a mixture of radioactive waste and cement. This toxic experiment formed the waste into gigantic putty-like blocks to store on the open prairie. The engineers succeeded as well as with their self-igniting fireproof rooms. Earth, air, fire, and water combined to turn the blocks into leaking tons of putty, the fire supplied by that insolent, non-conformist committee of beryllium, tritium, chromium, and the like. Once non-conforming chemical elements lay abandoned to the natural elements, the non-conformists combined into a somewhat self-igniting slow "fire" that melted into the soil to perfectly ruin another engineered solution. Now, the desert soil and the groundwater absorbed the poison, and surface ponds began to take on the supernatural "orange" glow.

    Not everyone failed to notice the miscreant behavior of Rockwell Int. in cahoots with the Department of Defense that leased Rocky Flats to the corporate giant. Private Enterprise and the U.S. Top Secret nuclear arms industry had created generations of an immoral and incestuous secret, resulting in a world-class environmental disaster. At least one safety engineer, Jim Stone, made a pest of himself by documenting spills, hazards, and environmental boo-boos. He audaciously reported the problems after his managers gave him an "all-clear to shut up," first by ignoring him, then by warnings, intimidation, and orders, until they fired him.

    "I was mad, damn mad. I knew it was illegal to shoot the bastards, so I went to the FBI instead."[82] Jim Stone, the frustrated former health and safety engineer, had gathered the evidence over six years from 1980 until 1986. He had written weekly reports identifying rampant safety violations. At first, his supervisors ignored him, but Stone kept writing reports and ruffling the feathers of Rockwell's well-oiled political flock of miscreants who supervised massive pollution at the nuclear bomb plant. Real corporate teammates should tow the company line. They kept secrets. They obeyed. Stone, the incorruptible iconoclast, continued his tortuous employment until management had enough of his intemperate reports and showed him the door.

Stone ratted out his polluting former employer to Denver's tabloid newspaper, *Westword*, which led to a special Grand Jury investigation, SGJ 89-2. In time, following the conclusions of the special grand jury and an indictment, the FBI performed a spectacular raid regarding the ongoing pollution at the nuclear bomb factory on the outskirts of Boulder.

In 1990, a photograph of Jim Stone appeared on the cover of Denver's *Westword*, that nosy, irreverent, popular Denver tabloid. The story inside the newspaper revealed him as the source who exposed the radioactive scandal. The news was reported a year and a half after that "spectacular" FBI raid. Stone, the former Rocky Flats Safety Engineer, appears with arms folded under a black hat, wearing a face full of some reasonable paranoia. A dimple sets firmly on his chin, and under the black hat and dark eyebrows, he looks grimly determined and tough as a mafioso enforcer. In the irony of "tabloid" versus the "traditional press," the Denver print and electronic opinion makers ignored the story. Without the gravitas of a major media outlet, a "tabloid" story of criminal conspiracy at the Top-Secret bomb plant was sensational but assumed to be baseless and untrue if the two Denver daily newspapers, *The Denver Post* and *The Rocky Mountain News*, hadn't headlined the story.

Jim Stone made serious allegations, and he had copied the records of health and safety violations known to DOE officials and Rockwell, Int.'s Rocky Flats managers. He made a better decision to hang the bastards by their own petards than shooting anyone. He claimed a Colossus of Rhodes-sized conspiracy among DOE officials and private enterprise employees who falsified records and ignored laws, consciously and criminally polluting the air and water of Colorado. The violations did not occur occasionally or accidentally. Rightfully or not, Stone said he "feared for his life."[83]

When the culprits at Rocky Flats called Haddon, Morgan & Foreman, the prosecution should have blinked. After all, these lawyers could figure out that the DOE knew about the crimes, that they ignored the dangerous conduct, and that Rockwell Int. ordered the crimes to continue to produce the triggers for nuclear weapons, which, so far, had never been used.

Prostitution of Justice

The intent of Rockwell Int. managers to enter into a criminal conspiracy erodes reasonable doubt into a politically indigestible decision. The former managers cried that they acted only as private employees at the bidding of, and under orders of, government officials to continue production and hide the waste. The DOE officials knew what they and Rockwell, Int. had done and would continue to do while they left it to their own self-interests.

Rockwell, Int., now attempted an engineered solution to the excess radioactive waste that Jim Stone, the whistleblower, told them would not work. Much like Rockwell's fireproofing project that set off a nuclear conflagration into the air, engineers came up with "pondcrete," a cancerous brew of nuclear offal and concrete. No one had tried the novel approach before, perhaps because it was unlikely that it would work. Estimating portions of concrete, radioactive offal, and water, they poured 1400-pound slabs of the putty-like glob that almost immediately began dissolving into the soil and water. The "pondcrete" pollutant did not much improve over the 55-gallon drums that had been dissolving, spilling their deadly contents over the years. The next less engineered option, to bury it, lay on the rack of the federal bureaucracy. A conglomeration of three-letter federal departments—EPA, DOE, DOD, DOJ, and DOT—had a radioactive cow to slaughter. No one knew a scientific solution other than to bury it. That would be fine absent the cluster of federal department lawyers conducting

Prostitution of Justice

interstate transportation contracts required to move the "yuk" to a burial site. No one in a private enterprise or any government agency wanted that kind of liability or publicity. And, of course, federal regulations and nuclear waste contracts prohibited the licensed nuclear dumping grounds in Utah or Nevada from accepting Rocky Flats' pondcrete.

As bad as the environmental pollution and cancer breeding at Rocky Flats was, a political farce began to bleed from within the Department of Justice. Ken Norton, the 10th U.S. District Attorney in Colorado, appointed by President George Bush, Sr., would have to prosecute those accused of committing the crime. In the interests of national defense (and very real profits for the manufacturer), the crime had essentially been forced upon Rockwell, Int.'s managers by Bush Administration officials. No palatable legal solution existed. The Bush Department of Justice (DOJ) must prosecute the Bush Department of Energy (DOE). U.S.D.A. Ken Norton swirled within the political quagmire. He shuffled along, trying to side-step the imbroglio until he ultimately refused to sign the indictment that SGJ 89-2 had produced.

Jim Stone, the whistleblower, had exposed Rockwell Int. to multi-billion-dollar penalties, as well as DOE officials and Rockwell Int. managers to personal criminal liabilities. Encrusted officials in both the corporation and the government faced consequences far beyond mere political disgrace or financial hardship. They now experienced the clutch in the stomach of a common criminal, their hearts thumping in real fear that they may wind up in a prison cell. The scandal grew such that even pitter-pats of alarm spooked the White House from the political fallout of those Big Shots facing criminal prosecutions.

Following the money led all the way to the kind of heavyweights too powerful to mourn the death of a snitch. Stone could only try to relax on his apartment porch, absorbing some sunshine, wondering if a CIA or other assassin held his image in a rifle's scope. Had he reached the end of international capitalist patience for his whistleblowing and document dump to *Westword*? Stone feared the wrath of the Bush 41 administration and secret black hat operations for having exposed cabinet members to potential criminal charges. Complicity and conspiracy accusations for covering up ongoing pollution under their control also made for lousy press.

In the interim, *Westword* did what tabloids do, continuing to investigate and verify the disgruntled employee's claims, exposing a massive environmental spill and scandalous cover up. *Westword* also ran a sidebar story asking for other whistleblowers to come forward.[84] Did they ever! Eventually, the mainstream media—The New York Times, The Los Angeles Times, even The *Denver Post,* and the *Rocky Mountain News*—published the scandal once the insignificant tabloid rag, *Westword,* rang the bell. Then came the civil actions. For Hal Haddon, who had watched Gary Hart's

Prostitution of Justice

presidential bid succumb to the truth that Gary Hart was cheating on his wife, as was revealed in the Miami Herald, the claims against his clients at Rocky Flats that were spread by *Westword* could only have been spawned in the same media gutters.

The Denver FBI Office had a Special Agent who had investigated and prosecuted environmental crimes, Jon Lipski. He worked in the Denver office. The December 1990 publication of the back story of the Rocky Flats raid and Stone's surreptitiously obtained documents didn't surprise the bespectacled, plain vanilla FBI agent. He appears with neat brown hair, average in height and weight, and a perfectly anonymous appearance, but he was bright, determined, and honest to a career-breaking fault.

Lipski had been dipping into Stone's claims of environmental crimes and the coverup for a year[85] before the June 6, 1989, Rocky Flats raid. He had begun with the approval of his inquiries, discreetly, in consultation with Ken Lemski, Deputy Assistant D.A. in the 10th U.S. Federal District Court with power to approve the initial investigation and access to a grand jury should the government need grand jury secrecy to protect the top-secret information of Rocky Flats. The FBI criminal division cooperated with the EPA to coordinate the investigation. Lipski knew that the fires of 1957 and 1969 at Rocky Flats originated in Building 771 from burning plutonium waste. Where there was fire, Lipski reasoned, there may still be smoke. The FBI worked in tandem with the EPA to conduct nighttime flights over Rocky Flats with heat-sensing infrared cameras. In confirmation of the Special Agent and his EPA infrared analysis expert, they had photographic proof of a heat signal in Building 771. The flight's EPA infrared analyst identified the heat signatures as those of burning nuclear waste. A supposedly closed retention pond also bore a heat signature, as well as a sewage spill that ran directly into two adjacent creeks, Woman Creek and Walnut Creek. The night-stalking surveillance flights gathered enough potential evidence of continuing environmental crimes to schedule two more nighttime aerial surveillance efforts. With three flights in two weeks' time, they found enough "smoke" to believe in fire. Lipski put two and two together to realize that the two previous fires were precursors to crimes that must be ongoing and that a third phosphoric/nuclear fire could occur.

Jon Lipski took his results to Ken Lemski, the ambitious prosecutor at the Department of Justice. Probable cause to indict Rockwell Int. or accuse the Department of Energy of complicity did not yet exist. If Lemski and Lipski wanted to make their case, they needed hard evidence. A few nights of infrared photography didn't reach the bar. A more intrusive approach, enforced with search warrants and Grand Jury secrecy, would take the lid off the case like a blue electrical flash before a nuclear explosion.

When the FBI conducted its raid on Rocky Flats, Hal Haddon was at his ranch in Archuleta County, way down in Southwestern Colorado. There, the San Juan and Rio Grande National Forests spread an umbrella of wilderness for wildlife, with mountain streams teeming with trout. Hal Haddon had loved fishing since he was a boy. By 1989, he could afford that spot of land, 275 miles from Denver, where he could relax. Once he found his ranch outside Pagosa Springs, Colorado, he purchased it under Beverly Haddon's name. On the day of the FBI raid, while Haddon fished, his office received a request from Rockwell Int.'s legal counsel, who found the firm in the telephone book. He asked if Haddon, Morgan & Foreman could help. The law firm responded en masse like a SEAL team on a counter-insurgency mission.

The firm's team drove north along the rolling foothills to rural Jefferson County, just south of Boulder, only to begin a two-hour security clearance procedure before being granted permission to enter the top-secret facility. The FBI's search went on for four days when phosphoric evidence that should have been illegally burned caught fire. Jim Stone may have sent some documents, and the FBI may have found some incriminating memorandums, even suspected burning under infrared surveillance, but then the search also produced Douglas Sanchini's diary: the Rocky Flats Plant Manager's diary. The

Prostitution of Justice

evidence in the diary caused the FBI to linger for another 14 days.

Operation Desert Glow turned up a morass of evidence against the businessmen, engineers, and political officials involved with Rocky Flats. The FBI removed 184 boxes filled with millions of documents and had to summon several trucks to haul the mother lode of environmental crimes down to Denver. There, the U.S. District Court would hold the raw ore in its vaults. Now, the prosecutors and the FBI needed a factory to mill the ore. For that, federal prosecutors turned to Merry Old England's Grand Jury, which codified and modified into 20th-century politically controlled and silenced citizens. Hal Haddon had the case right where he wanted it.

There were 3.5 million documents, 800 interviews, and 110 grand jury witnesses to put under oath, a tall order for any grand jury, but not too big for Special Federal Grand Jury (SGJ) 89-2, the first Special Grand Jury ever assembled in the 10th U.S. District Court. Hal Haddon recalls the case that would embroil his office in litigation for 20 years: The "Runaway Grand Jury," he seethed.[86]

Wes McKinley, the foreman of the grand jury, had a few things in common with Hal Haddon's father. He worked on the land as a dryland rancher and also as a schoolteacher. He wore his hard work on his jeans and couldn't give a hoot about a rattlesnake in a business suit, or he wouldn't have picked a fight

Prostitution of Justice

with the 10th U.S. District Court and Mike Norton, the U.S. District Attorney, nor President George Bush, nor Hal Haddon.

Rollie Rogers probably would have gotten along well with Wes, both growing up in rural Colorado counties, wearing cowboy hats and boots. Rogers tended to favor bolo ties with Cheyenne Indian red, white, and blue designs. McKinley wasn't as "cityfied" as the lawyer, mostly wearing a cowboy hat that covered his bald head, but he was all red, white, and blue at heart. Wes didn't have an office on any floor of any bank building to meet a Denver lawyer like the legendary Rollie Rogers or Hal Haddon. Instead, he asked a local lawyer[87] what a grand jury did when he received his notice to appear hundreds of miles away in Denver by mostly county roads.

McKinley had learned the basic idea of his duties in the Pledge of Allegiance, "freedom and justice for all," mixed in with rural country values of telling the truth and keeping his word. He joined twenty-three other grand jurors to listen to the evidence presented by an important lawyer from the government, prosecutor Ken Feinberg, and investigated by the famous FBI's Jon Lipski. The call of duty didn't care about the distances jurors must travel from throughout Colorado. The government they served paved the roads for them. The duty went on for 18 months. Federal Judge Sherman Finesilver had empaneled them and solemnly instructed them. The grand jurors had taken an oath. They must perform a public service if

Prostitution of Justice

they find evidence of a crime and indict those responsible. They must decide, not the lawyer presenting the case.

Politics and law thus intersected in the lives of Wes McKinley, the foreman of SGJ 89-2, and all the other jurors swallowed up in this environmental crime that scandalized the Department of Energy under the Bush White House. Ken Norton, a Republican colleague and former U.S. House Representative, carried the baggage of "political appointment" with experience in Administration but no working knowledge of criminal procedures or prosecutions. His career had left him far removed from the messy Constitutional protections that are the meat and potatoes of American Criminal Justice.

Hal Haddon loved all the portions of Justice Pie he could swallow when he baked it. Norton had foolishly placed his trust in an ambitious prosecutor and an FBI agent who tossed a political grenade he didn't know imperiled the President, powerful political patrons, and an enemy like Hal Haddon. Norton expected a nice, administratively handled, ham sandwich-like investigation and maybe an indictment, nothing too serious, and especially not any convictions of President George Bush's political appointments!

Ken Norton wandered the 10th U.S. District Courthouse oblivious to the downwind political radioactivity growing phosphorescent in SGJ 89-2. After two presidential terms of Ronald Reagan and the next, George Bush, few things on Hal Haddon's menu could please him more than fricasseed

Prostitution of Justice

Republicans. Lipski and Lemski had served up a banquet. Of course, Haddon could forego blowing up the Bush Administration with a scandalous prosecution within his inner circle for the sake of his client Rockwell Int. and its complicit managers. He could allow a few officials of the DOE to duck. The grand jury option may have occurred to the genius lawyer before he traveled from his ranch in Southern Colorado to Denver on the day of the raid: bury the case in the grand jury.

Hal Haddon had the Bush administration's Department of Justice targeting Republican allies in the Department of Energy in his sights. His office waded into the evidence, reviewing hundreds of thousands of documents and conducting its own investigation, which led to Washington D.C.

Haddon could feel comfortable in the backrooms of political power. He knew, supported, campaigned for, and represented the Big Dogs. He could pick up the phone and expect an answer from Gary Hart, Teddy Kennedy, or Bill Clinton. And soon, Ken Lemski would no longer have control of the case. The young federal prosecutor had stirred up a nest of snakes, and now Lemski was little more than a mouse caught by a political serpent.

By December 1990, Haddon, Morgan & Foreman had investigated the case thoroughly. It surely was a shame that DOD had expected delivery of all those nuclear weapons. Poor, isolated Rocky Flats needed the money to keep the shops clean, but the government had often been too stingy and neglectful.

Prostitution of Justice

True, it had gone on for 40 years in a faithful relationship between business and government. But the growing batches of environmental laws made for a confusing jumble of regulations. One could imagine a defense lawyer's discussion. You don't want to put someone in jail from Rockwell, Int., a patriotic corporation and political donor to the president, do you? And there's President Bush's Department of Defense. Will sending your president's political appointee to prison look good on a resume? Are you sure, Mr. Norton, that you want to prove your case? Wouldn't it just be easier to tell the grand jury to go home? Rockwell Int. feels very bad about all the pollution causing cancer and other illnesses. The corporation can generously offer $18.5 million in fines for a little cleanup. And remember, "Mum's the Word" about the future environmental damages and health risks. Let's not talk too much about the groundwater and worry folks who will be drinking it, bathing in it, and washing their hands. Okay?

Federal District Attorney Ken Norton, not surprisingly, pulled the plug on the grand jury's 18 months of work. Rockwell, Int. ultimately pleaded guilty to ten charges of violating federal hazardous waste disposal and clean water laws. Ambitious Asst. U.S. Atty. Kem Lemski woke up to smell the coffee with his career down around his ankles. Jon Lipski took another path, guided by Wes McKinley and followed by all the grand jurors who ran right into the fire.

Chapter Five: A Witch's Potion

The grand jurors had all sworn an oath. The word "oath" carries more weight than a politician's promise. They knew that the earth of the Rocky Flats property, rained upon, baked, and stirred, had grown into a 6,550-acre nuclear dumpsite and cancer incubator. Poison trickled through the soil into the drinking water. Wind carried the irradiated dust beyond all borders, down the front range of the Rocky Mountains to Albuquerque, New Mexico, and further to Arizona and into the atmosphere.

Wes McKinley had little enough water on his ranch in northeastern Colorado. Knowing that Rocky Flats had flagrantly continued to dump plutonium, a million times more toxic than uranium, grated against the values ingrained in him during his life. If he did not stand up, who would? When would it become too late, and the poison could not be abated? If their examination of the evidence required it and their signatures affirmed their decision, the U.S. Attorney should file an indictment. No one was above the law. Judge Sherman Finesilver had advised all the jurors of the service they must perform. Theirs was to make the hard decisions to indict if that is where the evidence pointed. It should have been simple for McKinley and the other members of SGJ 89-2, but politics, money, and power brewed a witch's potion.

Prostitution of Justice

Out on the Southeastern Colorado plains near Kansas and Nebraska, as far west as the Utah Border in Grand Junction, from the short grass to over 14,000-foot peaks, members of SGJ 89-2 met in Denver every two weeks for eighteen months. FBI Agent Jon Lipski had worked on the case. As far as McKinley was concerned, the decision wasn't difficult. They followed the instructions and found a slew of crimes, slow-smoked, that had soaked the prairie and into the groundwater.

By this time, the U.S.D.A.'s Ken Norton had gotten to know a tutor in Grand Jury Law. Hal Haddon had fought and filed grand jury indictments since Rollie Rogers lassoed him into the Public Defender's Office, and Dick Lamm had given him a full-ride scholarship in grand jury procedures through the Colorado Drug Enforcement Task Force. In Norton's other ear, the shouts of the Bush Administration, reminding him of his expected political loyalty, came through loud and clear. SGJ 89-2 will not bring indictments against career bureaucrats in the DOE nor managers of Rockwell, Int. They would receive immunity from prosecution and never have to testify. Pledges and oaths are for the little people to obey. Big Shots make the decisions. Ken Norton was only a political appointment, a man of ambition but no Big Shot.

The DOJ had determined that the sacrosanct DOE had directed the misconduct through Rockwell, Int. managers over the decades and would not be held responsible for DOE directions to break the law. They, nor DOE officials, would

Prostitution of Justice

suffer charges of false statements or conspiracy. In concert with burying the case in the grand jury, SGJ-89 would not be allowed to publish a report. What's the matter with a little glowing water under desert soil for all those nuclear-tipped missiles the national defense required, dirty or illegal? Sweep the investigation under a courthouse rug like so much nuclear waste buried at Rocky Flats.

Hal Haddon could kick up his heels and squeal with delight in a pasture of greenbacks. Rockwell Int.'s legal fees afforded Haddon, Morgan & Foreman a fresh look. The firm bought an enormous white mansion on Denver's Capitol Hill, which was once used as a Jewish Community Social Club. Located five blocks from Colorado's gold-domed capitol, the property on Lincoln St. came complete with a ballroom and swimming pool.

Not everyone felt the joy of Hal Haddon's miraculous legal accomplishment. Jim Stone may have blown a whistle and brought vigilance and fear of assassination upon himself for it. Wes McKinley, in his blue jeans and boots, and the others demanded to file a report, as the judge had told them they could do. His neighbors on the dry prairies had heard about the case and wondered openly what had happened. Had McKinley and the other jurors thrown the case? The mandated grand jury secrecy certainly made all those long, five-hour drives to and from Denver look fishy to neighbors and a waste of time to the grand jurors.

Prostitution of Justice

Horse Feathers! All the citizens of SGJ 89-2 stewed. The grand jurors had voted to file felony and misdemeanor charges against five Rocky Flats managers and three DOE officials. But, dang it, they did their sacred American duty, then got told to go home and shut up. That made every one of the jurors slapping mad, mad enough to face down the FBI, the U.S. District Court, and Hal Haddon's secret grand jury disposition sans "justice."

Hal Haddon now had his hands full with greenbacks over environmental lawsuits blowing over Rocky Flats, now a world-famous toxic nuclear site. The billable hours grew like teeth in crocodiles while friends from the law firm in Washington D.C. learned of the win without concern for secrets or how the dismissal of charges came to be. The DOD knew that Rockwell, Int., and later through EE&G, continued building nuclear triggers while making, spilling, and storing spent plutonium and its committee of related deadly elements ending in "ium." The plant would continue leaching its cancer-inducing vomit into the water and blowing slow-death plumes of radiated air over Denver, its suburbs, and beyond Colorado. EE&G, the DOD, DOE, and the Bush Administration became about as popular as 19th-century horse thieves to the environmentally conscious, duty-bound, and muzzled 20th-century citizens of Boulder.

Jon Lipski, now a pariah in the FBI, knew what would happen next. Before the DOJ could destroy his credibility and

Prostitution of Justice

his career, he took early retirement to begin working as a private investigator. SGJ 89-2 had formed relationships, sworn oaths together, voted their consciences and their duty, and they had relied on Lipski. He had gathered the evidence and explained it. He found and subpoenaed the 110 witnesses to testify. He dedicated more years of his life than the jurors had, all while wrestling with pigs in the federal bureaucracy who oinked "secrecy" like it meant justice.

No misdemeanors. No felonies. No fines. No jail. No personal responsibility. The muckety-mucks of business and government stood above the law. Their freedom had been ransomed from criminal jeopardy like middle-aged princes. Rockwell Int. must pay an $18.5 million fine and a tax write-off in a ledger. Hal Haddon, the Wizard of Laws, had paved a golden brick road and could tell Ken Norton, "That's how to run a grand jury!"

The pollution didn't stop when Rockwell Int. cut its losses and dropped the contract on December 31, 1989, tossing the bomb to defense contractor EG&G as of January 1, 1990. Wes McKinley knew the Walnut and Woman Creek wastes would enter the groundwater, which would absorb the poisonous pondcrete slabs from the prairies where they lay, decomposing. Wind would carry radiation-poisoned topsoil into the atmosphere to pollute the earth. For a man who worked the land with decent values, his one and one-half years of secret work in faraway Denver hadn't accomplished "diddly."

Prostitution of Justice

Up north, EE&G hadn't reported any three-eyed rattlesnakes or two-headed rabbits, but McKinley, Lipski, and the other jurors had heard enough of the lies about recovering the land or cleaning the water. Cancer kills people. The Rocky Flats airborne soil and groundwater pollution would cause cancer and kill people. It weighed on the conscience of SGJ 89-2. In 1992, twenty of the grand jurors signed on to a petition to release the Grand Jury Report that suffocated under lock and key in the vaults of the U.S. District Court.

McKinley couldn't sign on to the lie, and neither did Lipski nor the other jurors. They had already grown so agitated that McKinley made it his civil and patriotic duty to run for the Colorado House of Representatives as an Independent. Another grand juror, Ken Peck, a lawyer who had voted against the indictment, but who renounced the system that used them, agreed that the system had not worked as designed.

They found a bright, young, talented lawyer who would work on their case pro bono, the now famous Jonathan Turley. His first task was to battle the FBI's accusations of criminal conduct for the grand jurors' violation of their grand jury oath of secrecy. The high-stakes patriotic duty of these grand jurors could come at the cost of felony charges and potentially years behind bars at worst, and most certainly years of legal combat. Fortunately, those grand jury secrets had already been fought over and revealed in civil pleadings and testimony flowing

Prostitution of Justice

through state and federal courts from all the lawsuits now on file exposing the pollution in open records.

Right about then, Sherman Finesilver, the U.S. District Judge who had sealed the report, left the bench. Of course, as the old boy network would have it, an old acquaintance from Hal Haddon's days working bankruptcy cases at Davis, Graham, and Stubbs stepped in: Richard Matsch. Haddon's old acquaintance's judicial career had put him high on the hog of the 10th U.S. Federal District Court. He had worked his way out of the bankruptcy court to rule over the grand jury. This is the former bankruptcy referee who wanted Hal Haddon to explain his client's plight before accepting or rejecting a claim based on the lawyer's take on his client's character.

When the judge was younger, he professionally and sympathetically wondered how the lawyer's client had fallen into financial ruin and if his assets and liabilities pointed north in his moral compass. All these years later, those concerns for the honest citizens of SGJ 89-2 lacked the human luster of honest people representing truthful claims. Matsch would release a carefully edited report the grand jurors had submitted. Diplomacy and secrecy appeared to dance about in Judge Matsch's heart in his final words.

Yes, EE&G processed plutonium and slung it around just as criminally as Rockwell, Int. Moreover, the DOE and EE&G knew what they were doing, as they had when the FBI had raided Rocky Flats in 1989. The DOE still wanted bombs, but with all the bad press and nosey environmentalists, it had removed production from Rocky Flats and closed the plant permanently in 1992. All seemed done, and well done, at that.

Now, the damned runaway Grand Jury could ruin everything. All the bad press needed silencing. McKinley would leave the carcass of Rockwell, Int. on the table while exposing the very dirty secret that the cancer factory at Rocky Flats had continued to the rhythm of a full-tilt Western Boogey "in the interest of national security." The conduct of that runaway grand jury defied everything SGJ 89-2 had uncovered and hoped to accomplish.

Like cottonmouths in a swamp, a censored report bobbed to the surface and was released in 1993 through persistent legal pleading and disturbing press leaks. That report made Wes McKinley and the others wearing the Court's muzzle as mad as when Finesilver refused to release the report in the first place. Judge Matsch had tossed the work of McKinley, Lipski, and the grand juror members outside the courthouse like an abandoned litter of puppies.

Judge Matsch unexpectedly started a fight. He didn't mean to do so as much as he apparently came to believe that a little lying by omission should calm the storm. He could have done the right thing and released the entire unvarnished report, including EE&G's radioactive warts. He never imagined Wes McKinley, nor any other SGJ-89-2 jurors, had still more fight left in them. He may have realized they came because duty

Prostitution of Justice

called, but so much duty offended his judgment. They came because some Big Dogs in government and industry broke the law in their humble, unlearned opinion. McKinley, Lipski, and the rest of the jurors had as sizable a fight in them as did their lawyer, Jonathan Turley, who has since become a national beacon of constitutional law and somewhat of a talking head whom the press love.

In 1996, following a brutal legal battle, Turley first defended against an indictment of his clients. The dam broke, and SGJ-89-2 won. Matsch ordered the unredacted report to the public. That made a good start, even though it had done nothing about the already ruined earth, air, and water. When the furnaces stopped, the sludge gathered in rivulets and had been sprayed atop the prairies. The pondcrete, which no nuclear site in the nation was licensed to store or bury, cast a shadow like the Enola Gay over Hiroshima. The groundwater is soaked into cancerous sewage. Had we learned nothing from Nagasaki?

For a man, a third-generation dryland rancher, the drip of outright lies, half-truths, and secret crimes had gone on long enough. First, Wes McKinley collaborated with Lipski, another grand juror, and a Lawyer to reveal the original grand jury findings. Next, he campaigned for election to the Colorado House of Representatives on a platform of honesty in government, a novel idea. He was defeated but not deterred. McKinley, like any good cowboy, got back on the horse and

Prostitution of Justice

mounted his second campaign in 2004, running as a Democrat and winning.

That year, the Runaway Grand Jury Hal Haddon legally coiled around and smothered recovered from the venom of silence. Lipski, McKinley, and grand Juror Jacque Brever, with their lawyer, Carol Balkan, published The Ambushed Grand Jury: How the Justice Department Covered Up Government Nuclear Crime: And How We Caught Them Red Handed.

Wes McKinley, cowboy, math teacher, and honest citizen, won. He took public office with the microphone the voters had granted him. Now, he runs with the Big Dogs.

Following the swearing-in ceremony at the Colorado Capitol on January 5, 2005, the new Colorado State House Representative, along with former FBI Agent Jon Lipski, grand juror Jacque Brever, and their lawyer, Carol Balkan, leveled a 16-page internet broadside to expose the public health and safety risks to anyone stepping onto the wasteland made of Rocky Flats.

McKinley's voice and the patriotic choir of SGJ 89-2 came out of the wilderness, setting a community prairie fire over the aging coverups and crimes. They spilled enough dirty laundry to fill a Stygian stable for a Herculean wash. Wes McKinley served in the Colorado Statehouse from 2005 until 2013. The DOE deeded the land at Rocky Flats to the U.S. Fish & Wildlife Services in 2007 for a National Park.

Chapter Six: The Wizards of Laws

Hal Haddon loved Colorado all the way down to his feet. He wore cowboy boots to court and owns a ranch near Pagosa Springs. He loves nature, mountains, and fishing. He had farmed through his childhood and understood the value of land. His work putting people in prison while in charge of the Colorado Drug Task Force and his career in private practice with a motto of "Reasonable Doubt for a Reasonable Fee" provided him with a wizard's understanding of both sides of the courtroom. It also allowed him the life of a gentleman rancher in his beloved Colorado with "mountains like pyramids."

In contrast, Wes McKinley wore cowboy boots and hats because he grew up wearing boots and a broad-brimmed hat as a third-generation Colorado cowboy. Haddon, on the other hand, had spent his entire adult life in the realms of power, lawyers and judges, congressmen, and senators, and even President Bill Clinton, as his firm handled Clinton's tax matters. Haddon had to grow up with grit and gravel in his belly, but no one could rope a jury or shape public opinion like the Wizard of Laws.

Hal Haddon could dress like a man from the land on his ranch or a sportsman when he went fishing. Men like Wes McKinley did more than dress the part. He lived the part and walked the walk all the way from his ranch through two

Prostitution of Justice

elections, inspired by a failed grand jury system. It took rare strength for Wes McKinley, Jon Lipski, and the SGJ 89-2 jurors to school Hal Haddon in justice and to expose an inside fix of the grand jury.

Rocky Flats landed on the EPA's National Priorities List in 1989. Public interest in the environment had replaced Cold War sentiments for nuclear warheads. The DOD ordered fewer triggers. A glance at the change in political leadership from Bush to Clinton explains the interest in a peacetime economy with the fall of the Berlin Wall and Russia in financial and political decline prior to Vladimir Putin's rise to power.

Some doubt entered the minds of environmental activists that "reasonable doubt" or personal responsibility exists for international corporations. The Big Shots seemed to receive the justice money buys. Frustrated citizen groups and their lawyers delivered bouquets of banknotes by filing environmental lawsuits that Haddon, Morgan & Foreman expertly defended with inexhaustible billable hours. There, the pleadings, the correspondence, and drawers of investigation and research waited for sorting to age until the math worked and a reasonable settlement, or trial, was reached.

The world knew Haddon, Morgan & Foreman. The slogan of the Denver law firm, "Reasonable Doubt for a Reasonable Fee," understated its skill and power. John and Patsy Ramsey paid a reasonable fee when doubt had entered the minds of Boulder P.D. on the morning of December 26, 1996.

Prostitution of Justice

Boulder P.D. had not been tasked to find reasonable doubt at the home of John Ramsey but rather probable cause.

It seemed odd that the parents had separated themselves, Patsy in the sunroom and John in his office. Questioning would have to wait while Commander John Eller ignored suspicious circumstances out of his reverence for "credible millionaires." In the Ramseys' defense, they had a right to refuse questioning without an attorney under the Supreme Court ruling in Miranda v. Arizona from 1966. Certainly, no police interview would occur once Haddon, Morgan & Foreman was retained until the law firm said so.

Unexpectedly, SGJ 89-2 had recoiled, rattled, and struck venom into political abuse of grand jury secrecy. The Federal statute had failed to stop unsophisticated rubes from leaking or writing reports even when told not to do so. Haddon had prosecuted drug lords and drug mules under a similar Colorado statute. If the grand jury law in Colorado that mirrored the federal statute remained unaltered, another runaway grand jury could ambush the tightly woven narrative espoused by the defense of an intruder. The right to issue a report and the right to free speech of the grand jurors may have to be adjusted to protect the reputations of John and Patsy Ramsey from accusations and bad press.

Legislators and legislation are known to move at glacial speeds even when a need or issue in society attracts the interest of the public and comes to the attention of policymakers. The

Prostitution of Justice

will to make changes for the health, safety, and protection of the public moves the new law at a measured pace through debate, discussion, and public comment until it reaches legislative votes. The proposed law must be drafted, and committees argue for changes, deletions, and improvements. Reports must come out. Debates follow. Changes are made. Witnesses and public hearings add to or subtract from the new bill. Finally, having made it through the House of Representatives or the Senate, the new law goes to the other chamber to make its suggestions and incorporate those changes into yet another review for final reconciliation.

Depending on the urgency of a new law, a change can take several years. If the appetite of the public or a particularly powerful lobby must be satiated, a single legislative session will suffice. In the matter of "reforming" the responsibilities of grand jurors by adding a felony criminal penalty for publicly leaking deliberations or testimony, the glacial pace of the bill to silence grand jurors and witnesses moved like Icelandic lava over ice after the murder of JonBenet Ramsey.

It took only two weeks in legislative chambers to "fix" Colorado's grand jury statute in favor of secrecy. Immediately after swearing in the new legislature, a corrective bill to change the law entered the Colorado House of Representatives on January 8, 1997, thirteen days after JonBenet had been murdered. Some digression may explain the school of grand

Prostitution of Justice

jury procedures Haddon, Morgan & Foreman practiced within the brain trust of the partnership.

Norman R. Mueller graduated from Yale Law School in 1974, passed the Colorado Bar, and began working in the Colorado Public Defender's Office. There, he saved clients with his research and writing skills when choreographed street fights transformed into courtroom brawls resulting in a guilty verdict. His search through trial transcripts and law argued for certainty that all the rules were followed. Convictions must be "fair and square." Disobedience to the rules could turn on objections raised, jury instructions, and the exact meaning of statutes, dependent on how the judge had dealt with the jurors, witnesses, and attorneys. Trials with unsatisfactory results turn courtroom decisions into papered battlefields.

Norm Mueller could juggle courtroom dramas full of whirling *Globe*s of legal theories into tangible arguments. He wrote a chapter in the Colorado Appellate Handbook and published a scholarly article in The Colorado Lawyer on "Grand Jury Abuse" as recently as 1988, the year before SGJ-89-2 assembled. Mueller had practiced with Lee Foreman before they joined Haddon and Morgan. Mueller's brilliance was then absorbed into the brain trust. Mueller also taught at the University of Colorado Law School.

Norm Mueller understood grand jury practice from both a practical and scholarly point of view. Many criminal charges come from grand jury inquiries, especially in dicey situations

Prostitution of Justice

and decisions where political implications exist that a district attorney may wish to avoid. The sooner the practitioner understands the procedures, legislative terms, and limitations of the grand jury, the more able the defense.

Given the experience and brilliance of the law firm employed by John Ramsey, a grand jury strategy would demand contemplation in the opening moments of engagement. Equally so, given the initial dithering of Alex Hunter, the delay of an arrest allowed time to prepare an impenetrable defense. DAs face political ramifications, but private lawyers don't. Time also figures into legal strategies. Grand juries take time with proceedings conducted in secrecy while the public passion for justice, or appetite for "blood," diminishes.

Alex Hunter's bluster days after the murder, "We know who you are," soon began to fade, and citizens expressed their outrage at Hunter's ineptitude, corruption, or both. The DA once enjoyed the attention of the press, scandalously releasing information to Lawrence Schiller for his book *Perfect Murder, Perfect Town* and giving tips to reporters he liked, like Craig Lewis of the *Globe*. He curried favor with the tabloid editor with inside tidbits of the case and tossed an occasional bone of where to look for an interview. His office split between charging the Ramseys, waiting for a confession, or a "silver bullet" of proof of an intruder. Hunter did not dither when it came to blaming Boulder P.D. for fumbling the investigation by not providing him with "Probable Cause," even if that

Prostitution of Justice

determination fell on Hunter's own shoulders. Gangs of reporters wanted information, to know if the parents would be charged or any other information that would make a headline.

The case had become politically "uncomfortable," with Haddon, Morgan, and Foreman representing John Ramsey. Grand juries made a perfect closet to keep the secrets of a far-reaching or flawed investigation. Surely a runaway grand jury or grand juror who would speak outside of the secret proceedings was not in Hunter's calculations.

Haddon, Morgan, and Foreman had a belly full of Wes McKinley and his ilk from the Rocky Flats debacle and moved in sync with potential legislation to put the kibosh on a leaky grand jury proceeding.

Like a premonition, a bill to change Colorado's Grand Jury Rules had come to the attention of the Colorado District Attorneys' Council. It was discussed with legislators during a conference in the summer of 1996.[88] The council had drafted a proposed new statute (16-5-205.5 C.R.S. "Grand Jury Reports") in late 1996. Then, on January 8, 1998, two weeks, yes, TWO WEEKS, after the JonBenet Ramsey murder and mystery began, Senator Ed Perlmutter, a Democrat, and Representative Bill Kaubman, a Republican, submitted to the Colorado Legislature a new bill to "silence" grand jurors.

That bill, HB 97-1009, changed the procedures and circumstances under which a grand jury issued a report. Those changes would incorporate certain prohibitions preventing jurors or witnesses from making public the testimony before the grand jurors or deliberations. This change silenced a grand juror from discussing the JonBenet Ramsey investigation, or any other grand jury case, thus committing all the evidence to eternal grand jury secrecy. The change to the old law passed on March 21, 1997. Governor Roy Roemer signed it into law on April 8, 1997. Now, all Alex Hunter had to do was "dance" while keeping the secret that he would not be pressing any charges naming John or Patsy Ramsey.

But there was a catch, a common one. Laws do not take effect immediately, and this new grand jury "gag order" would not apply to grand juries sworn in before October 1, 1997. To complicate matters, the next statutorily assembled Boulder Grand Jury, the one to be silenced under the new law, would not convene until April 1998. Through all this legal muscle and blubber, Alex Hunter would have to "dance," pretending that the case remained under "investigation."

When Hal Haddon ran grand juries for the Colorado Crime Strike Force, district attorneys he worked with made every cooperative decision based upon the political reality on the ground. The law, then in effect, needed clarification at the time of the Ramsey case to preserve secrecy by revising a part of the statute then in place.

The new language suggested by the Colorado District Attorney's Council provided a legislative roadmap for when and how to release a grand jury's findings in cases of inconclusive results, i.e., no charges. It exalted protections for witnesses, allowing the subpoenaed citizen to access the testimony and object to its release. The intent of the new legislation was to protect the public from police or a government servant's wrongdoing while protecting the accused from public humiliation. Bill Ritter, Denver District Attorney and future Governor of Colorado, argued for the change to the legislature, conspicuously supported by Bob Grant, Jim Peters, and Dave Thomas in Adams, Arapahoe, and Jefferson Counties. They would compose the metropolitan Denver "Dream Team" of prosecutors who were supposed to aid Alex Hunter in the search for JonBenet's killer. With the empanelment of a grand jury, the various District Attorneys could offer advice without risking public scrutiny, while gagged citizens would assume anonymous and silenced responsibility.

The new law could not take effect for a year for the Ramsey case to end well for the defense. Acting as the front man for the sideshow, Alex Hunter promised justice, a better investigation by Lou Smit, a trial if that's what he must, all the way up to and until seating of the Boulder Grand Jury in April 1998.

When the grand jury finished its work and voted to indict John and Patsy Ramsey for Child Abuse Resulting in Death and Conspiracy, Hunter refused to sign the indictment. Instead, he held a press conference to advise that no charges would be filed and that he had never been so proud of his country. Thirteen years later, the truth came out that there had been an indictment. By then, mythologies and accusations against an invisible intruder had consumed the facts. The great debate argued that either an intruder did it or the parents did it. Like a high school debate, sides would be taken, points and counterpoints made, an occasional ribbon awarded, and everyone goes home to dinner, except for JonBenet Ramsey.

Chapter Seven: Aftermath

Long before JonBenet Ramsey became synonymous with unsolved mysteries, unproven theories, and unfulfilled justice in the foothills of Boulder, Steve Thomas had hung up his badge. His resignation from Boulder P.D. freed him to work with *Vanity Fair's* Ann Louise Bardach for the inside story. Some say Bardach's "scoop" cost $100,000, and it was worth it in circulation and prestige.

Ramsey proceeded to file a lawsuit against Thomas and *Vanity Fair*. Much earlier, after the breakup of the friendship between the Ramseys and the Whites in Atlanta at JonBenet's funeral, the slur of "child murderer" slimed Fleet White and, by association, his wife Priscilla and children, Fleet Jr. and Daphne. Thomas's citizen friend, Fleet White, who joined the cop in his suspicions of the parents' involvement in JonBenet's horrible death, would become clickbait. He and his family would be savaged across the internet.

In that once comfortable home of Fleet and Priscilla White near Chautauqua Park, war drums pounded. Former best friend John Ramsey's accusation that Fleet White had murdered JonBenet Ramsey harpooned Fleet White and his professional reputation. The truth is that neither Steve Thomas nor Boulder P.D. seriously considered Fleet White as a suspect but did see him as a witness.

Prostitution of Justice

Although he didn't dress, speak, or pretend like a cowboy, Fleet White had learned from somewhere how to "cowboy up." He didn't rely on tabloids, read tea leaves, or hire a handwriting expert to ferret out the political intrigue that had removed the case from criminal justice. He watched and saw the American tradition in sensitive cases to reduce the critical inquiry to matters of favor and intrigue.

White enjoyed years of family friendship with the Ramseys. They had sailed together, chummed around, and shared travel and dinners as families. JonBenet was his daughter Daphne's best friend. Fleet and Priscilla had to balance those experiences with the bizarre events at the Ramsey home, the appearance of JonBenet's corpse the morning after Christmas, and the "tabloid" behavior of John and Patsy at the Atlanta funeral. He searched his soul and let his conscience guide his insights into John Ramsey's calm, courteous, professional demeanor. Despite all their close associations with the Ramseys, Fleet and Priscilla White could not help but entertain the dreadful possibility that JonBenet's death was not the act of an intruder and perhaps not a mystery to the family.

Fleet White's father was an oil man, a breed that would explore a desert, a tundra, or an ocean. Fleet followed that profession but had to leave the occupation, or more accurately, was forced off his work, because of the accusations and cruel publicity surrounding JonBenet Ramsey's sickening murder. With unwanted free time to read, reflect, and respond to his undeserved position as a social pariah, he didn't have to travel far to explore the remarkably powerful relationship of Hal Haddon with law, politics, and the candidates for power, including the Colorado District Attorneys Council, Colorado's House of Representatives, Senate, and related elected power players, to include Colorado Governor Roy Romer.

A year after the Ramsey investigation began, on December 18, 1997, Fleet, accompanied by Priscilla, met with Governor Romer, Colorado's most powerful elected person in the orbit of Hal Haddon's political party. The Whites reported their skepticism of Boulder authorities, more specifically of the D.A.'s office and Alex Hunter. The Whites feared politics would play a trump card in denying an arrest or trial of JonBenet's killer if Romer did not appoint a special prosecutor. The busy Governor soon responded that he would not intervene in the JonBenet Ramsey investigation, principally because he did not believe the police investigation had been completed, nor had Boulder P.D. referred the case to the Boulder D.A.'s office for prosecution.

The Whites felt as though their communication with the Governor had been dismissed, nor did they believe that waiting for Boulder P.D. to continue its investigation would overcome the obstacle within Hunter's office that had so far failed to support the efforts of the police department. The Whites stated in a letter to the editor of the Boulder *Daily Camera* that they continued to hope that Governor Romer would intervene and

Prostitution of Justice

stop the bickering between Boulder P.D. and the Boulder D.A.'s office. Hope reigned eternally in the Christian hearts of Fleet and Priscilla White, to no avail.

Following the Whites' gubernatorial dismissal, a funny thing happened to the Ramsey case on its way to the grand jury, if one finds amusement in backroom politics. With the revised grand jury law of forced secrecy awaiting the required amount of statutory time before taking effect, Alex Hunter's blustering promises of justice before the cameras ended. He never again claimed to know who the perpetrator was. He dawdled in his office, approving plea bargains and pursuing the paths of least resistance, never pressuring his staff of excellent plea-bargaining Assistant D.A.s to expand their skills by going to trials. He did spend a lot of time visiting with journalists. Craig Lewis, the *Globe* editor, frequented Hunter's office.

After hiring Lou Smit as a special investigator, ostensibly to review the work of Boulder P.D., Hunter stepped back from public commentary until he could rely on some "reasonable" doubt by pointing to Lou Smit's intruder theory. Meanwhile, Boulder P.D. ran down every possible suspect and witness, checked backgrounds, and continued interviews while running up an overbudget of a million dollars in man-hours, but failed to find an intruder, a suspect, or a means of regaining its pride.

Hunter had found some journalists willing to choreograph his dance of finding justice for JonBenet with his

Prostitution of Justice

denial that Boulder P.D. had identified any plausible suspects. That reckless, religious, and obstinate "cowboy," Steve Thomas, had resigned after snatching the secrets of the investigation from police files. This opened the opportunity for him to leave Boulder P.D. to sell the story and author his book. That left the rest of Boulder P.D. and the lawyers in the D.A.'s office to endure the release of their mutual animosities and theories, leaked as if from paper bags of water, and all of it so much wasted effort.

The fettered Boulder P.D. was out on a limb. They had worked diligently, if somewhat overwhelmed, providing what they discovered to a prosecution that did not want it. In time, they sought legal guidance for their next step outside of Hunter's Dance Studio. In July 1997, Boulder attempted a fresh approach to fighting crime. They accepted the pro bono services of three respected Colorado defense lawyers who offered their services.

Daniel Hoffman was the youngest Manager of Safety ever for the City and County of Denver, a criminal defense and corporate lawyer, and a part-owner of the Denver Nuggets Basketball Team. He graduated from the University of Denver Law School and was later Professor Emeritus and Dean of his law school alma mater. He marched with Dr. Martin Luther King and worked with Hal Haddon on the Robert F. Kennedy presidential campaign. Haddon also represented Hoffman in a litigation case filed against him by Sherman & Howard, Hoffman's former law firm.

The second of the triumvirate of volunteer lawyers, Robert N. Miller, graduated from the University of Colorado Law School in 1965. He went on to serve as the District Attorney of Weld County, Colorado, and as the United States District Attorney for Colorado before serving as Chief Counsel for US West. He represented both individuals and corporations through all stages of government investigations and white-collar crime cases, with much experience in internal investigations and compliance matters. Miller and Haddon had previously worked together in civil litigation and appeals.

Richard N. Baer, the third of the expert legal minds, attended Duke University Law School, Hal Haddon's alma mater, and began his career in Brooklyn, New York, as a homicide prosecutor. Following this work in the criminal courts, Baer showed up in Colorado to work for the firm of Sherman & Howard, where he headed up the firm's litigation department. He had also worked extensively in corporate law, serving as General Counsel for Liberty Media, Executive Vice President, and Chief Legal Counsel for United Health Group, and formerly held the same positions for Quest Communications, Inc.

All this legal horsepower gave the public hope that their experience and "learned" advice would help solve Boulder P.D.'s baffling investigation and evidence problems. The uninformed public could hope that no matter where the evidence should lead, whether to a family member or an intruder, the mystery would reach a resolution, perhaps even to an arrest. However, Hal Haddon tended to engineer planned results, and these three lawyers had close ties to the first-named partner of Ramsey's defense firm.

Mr. Baer's former law firm, Sherman & Howard, represented Lockheed Martin, the purchaser of John Ramsey's Access Graphics. In fact, Sherman & Howard also represented Access Graphics during Ramsey's tenure as owner in a dispute with a terminated employee. Robert Miller and Hal Haddon worked together on a civil case reported to have been worth a juicy $15 million.

The relationship of these three "volunteers" who offered their assistance to the baffled, muzzled, and ambushed Boulder P.D. reeks of the likely inside relationships between the "volunteers" and Hal Haddon, a world-class power broker, lawyer, and political mastermind. Of course, Hoffman, Miller, and Baer offered all the assistance they felt reasonable while the pages of the calendar turned, the clock ticked, and Alex Hunter awaited the lapse of each tick of the second hand. Hopefully, the public's memory of the gooey ingredients that had opened the volunteer assistance would lapse. With all that time, the recipe necessary to impanel a muzzled grand jury without statutory authority to report its deliberations would have been baked. Alex Hunter could then refuse to sign the indictment of

John and/or Patsy Ramsey that grand jury members might sign and would be prohibited from discussing.

Try as they did, these legal powerhouses of the triumvirate of Daniel Hoffman, Robert N. Miller, and Richard N. Baer couldn't help Boulder P.D. find the probable cause to make an arrest. And, finally, on August 12, 1998, Alex Hunter could stop dancing. The clock had run out on the former grand jury statute, and the silencing of the jurors could ensue. Hunter never did show much rhythm or grace in his weak-kneed surrender to an American giant of law and political strongman, Harold A. Haddon. In fact, within a fortnight of JonBenet's murder, the Boulder D.A. ended his bluster, crawled into his office to accept his defeat, and fed off an occasional "Attaboy" news story from a tabloid journalist fishing for a favor that would lead to a scoop.

Although some of his Assistant D.A.s may have wanted to see charges filed against the parents, others shunned the idea, knowing that finding proof beyond a reasonable doubt against the Haddon, Morgan, and Foreman law firm would require a miracle almost equal to raising JonBenet from the dead. Hunter accepted his circumstances like a child accepting a parent's command, "Go to your room!" He tossed the statutorily contrived confabulation to the grand jury, summoned under the new language of C.R.S. 16-5-205, and retired at the end of his term, ending his twenty-eight-year career as Boulder County District Attorney. Records from a local video rental store show

Prostitution of Justice

him exorcising his failure of duty in the JonBenet Ramsey case with X-rated films such as "White Cotton Panties."

Hunter's political decision to forsake justice and abandon the memory of JonBenet to a muzzled grand jury didn't fool Fleet White. He quit playing the fool after JonBenet's Atlanta funeral. His first step, speaking to Governor Roemer, backfired. Roemer was part of the political party cabal in Colorado and subject to Hal Haddon's influence or advice if called upon. The press had hardly taken notice of Fleet White's unusual request for a special prosecutor with his wife, Priscilla. After all, Fleet White was a suspect at one time, even though cleared by Boulder P.D.

The grand jury foil had made fools of Boulder P.D. and a trusting public. Haddon had brilliantly utilized his intensive investigation methods with the appointment of Lou Smit as a special investigator, independent of Boulder P.D., to materialize an intruder, the alternate suspect needed to raise doubt, reasonable or not, before the jury.

In the decades after the 1963 Supreme Court case of Gideon v. Wainwright, which brought the right to a lawyer to the criminal justice system, justice had metastasized, often proving to be an illusion for the poor defendant too intimidated by the legal system to demand a trial. Miranda v Arizona, the right to remain silent and to have a lawyer present for questioning, raised an invaluable standard of protection against high-pressure confessions but still required a suspect strong-

Prostitution of Justice

willed enough to demand a lawyer. John and Patsy Ramsey both had the good fortune of being seen as "Credible Millionaires" and invited an attorney to their house on the morning of December 26, 1996, who advised their silence and recommended Bryan Morgan of Haddon, Morgan, and Foreman as counsel.

Fleet White reminded some of John Wayne: tall and rangy, a good guy and honest, and not a poor man. Still, it costs time, money, and bottomless strength to stand in the fight. When the soldiers protecting the settlers abandon the wagon train and sell whiskey to the warriors who set fire to the wagons while taking scalps, even heroes must retreat. Yachts and the Boulder lifestyle could have continued to offer Fleet and his family "the good life" if only Fleet and Priscilla would surrender their beliefs and leave their consciences to the morass. Just shut up. Wilt. Be good sheep. Enjoy the rainbows. The Whites, however, were not sheep nor fooled, nor would Fleet chew cud any more than John Wayne wore glass slippers.

The potential for charges and an arrest or a lawsuit from hell dragged most of the speculation about the parents into a graveyard, as planned. Steve Thomas was sued. Fleet White is still dragged through the mud on the internet. The relationship between Thomas and White grew from professional to personal respect. John and Patsy Ramsey could fill a phone book with suspects, but Fleet White was never a serious suspect in the eyes of Steve Thomas, Boulder P.D., nor rational onlookers. Fleet

Prostitution of Justice

White had never studied law or mastered the complexities of political science in shaping public opinion, nor had he built his career in tandem with the state and national political power of governors, senators, presidential candidates, and even a President, Bill Clinton. White's political experience occurred mostly at PTA and school board meetings in Boulder.

The Ramseys' interview on CNN on January 1, 1997, had infuriated the Whites as a "tabloid" stunt, and the press coverage of the Memorial in Boulder exposed them and their children as camera fodder. The false accusation of murdering and sexually torturing the corpse of a child excoriated White professionally. He lost. He lost faith in justice for JonBenet but not in God or his family. He didn't have the Machiavellian skills of Hal Haddon, but he had more raw guts than John Ramsey could fit in a teabag and enough brains and determination to expose how he believed retribution for JonBenet's death had been manipulated and the law "rigged" to silence the Boulder Grand Jury.

After October 13, 1999, twenty months following the first headlines when Alex Hunter addressed the press to announce that there would be no charges in JonBenet's death, the investigation all but died, and the mythology began. The Whites soldiered on with a second letter to the press, which was noticed when the *Denver Post* published it, and a recap made it into the *New York Times*. The letter laid out the entire sordid political gamesmanship in a scheme to delay "justice" long enough to make a whore of the legislature, the district attorney's office, and the main persons who had an interest in dismantling the murder investigation. No one in that brothel cared.

No one with any power to dispute the outcome of the grand jury listened to or acted on Fleet White's call of honor. His search for truth would wait for thirteen years before the truth was uncovered, and that the grand jury had indeed voted to indict John and Patsy Ramsey for Child Abuse Resulting in Death and Conspiracy. A charge is just a charge, and the Ramseys remain innocent until they are proven guilty. Rest assured that it will never occur before a judge and jury. Haddon, Morgan & Foreman performed one of the most amazing acts of criminal defense in the history of the United States of America, proving reasonable doubt can be found on the auction block. The case polished the golden career of one of the United States of America's greatest lawyers from any century. He immediately saw the need to change a troublesome law in his path to victory for his clients. Hal Haddon had the power of a medieval prince and has since retired to his ranch outside of Pagosa Springs, Colorado. He has been seen at a Crime Con in Denver, Colorado, in 2025 with the still innocent until proven guilty, John Ramsey.

Fleet and Priscilla White survived. They held on and came back to raise Fleet, Jr., and their daughter, Daphne. Both of their children graduated from the United States Naval Academy, a noble institution that accepts only the best. And that proves the quality of their upbringing, no matter the snipes of internet ghouls. As for the lawyers, Machiavelli admonishes in his masterpiece, The Prince, "Hence it is necessary for a prince wishing to hold his own to know how to do wrong, and to make use of it or not according to necessity."

Prostitution of Justice

Craig Lewis, Globe Editor

Prostitution of Justice

J.T. Colfax, Agit Prop artist

Fleet White, former Ramsey family friend.

Prostitution of Justice

Carol McKinley, Fox News

Prostitution of Justice

All photos provided are copyrighted by Judith Phillips Photography. Visit her website at judithphillipsphotography.com.

ENDNOTES

[1] John and Patsy Ramsey, *The Death of Innocence*, New American Library, New York, 2000, p. 12

[2] as with Don Davis, *JonBenet Inside the Ramsey Murder Investigation*, St. Martin's Press, New York, 2000, pg. 54.

[3] Detective Linda Arndt, *Good Morning America*, ABC, September 13, 1998.

[4] Thomas, Steve, *JonBenet: Inside the Ramsey Murder Investigation*, pp.26-29.

[5] Howard Pankratz, "Killer Wiped Body," *The Denver Post*, February 5, 1997.

[6] Interview with John and Patsy Ramsey, CNN, "Early Prime," Brian Cabell, January 1, 1997.

[7] Alan Folsom, *The Day After Tomorrow* (New York: Warner Books, New York, 1994).

[8] Colorado Revised Statutes, Title16, Criminal Proceeding, §16-3-102

[9] Todd Hartmann, "Standing in her Shoes," *The Rocky Mountain News*, May 5, 2001, 17a.

[10] Hartmann, "Standing in her Shoes,"18.

[11] Chuck Green, "Smit's Theory a Stale Story," *Denver Post*, May 7, 2001, p.1, sec. B.

[12] Smit claims that marks on the back and face of JonBenet Ramsey's corpse came from an Air Taser stun gun. Police state the unexplained abrasions may have come from a button or snap. The manufacturer denies the claim.c

Prostitution of Justice

[13] Don Gentile and David Wright, editors, JonBenet, the Police Files, American Media, Inc., Boca Raton, Florida, pg. 399, 2003.

[14] John and Patsy Ramsey, The Death of Innocence, New American Library, New York, 2000, p. 146.

[15] Hodges, A Mother Gone Bad, pp. 1-4

[16] Ibid. pp. 6.

[17] Others, Lou Smit and John Douglas, suggest the note's length, fantastical quality combined with a distraught emotional state of a person who just committed a murder, must have been written at leisure, before the murder, by an "intruder," waiting for the Ramseys to come home from the White's Christmas party.

[18] Boulder Daily Camera, August 6, 1998.

[19] Newsweek, "The Intruder Theory," May 19, 2000.

[20] Good Morning America, ABC News, January 15, 2021.

[21] The Reporters committee for Freedom of the press, "Ramsey family defamation case dismissed," January 10, 2005, https://www.rcfp.org/ramsey-family-defamation-case-dismissed.

[22] Charlie Brennan, "When the System Falls Short," The Rocky Mountain News, December 18, 2001.

[23] Ibid.

[24] Interview, Patsy and John Ramsey. CNN, "Early Prime," Brian Cabell, January 1, 1997.

[25] Interview, Lou Smit, NBC News, "Good Morning America, Katie Curic, April 30, 2001.

[26] Time Magazine, Richard Woodbury, and Jeffrey Shapiro, "Crime: Did an Intruder Kill JonBenet Ramsey," October 25, 1999.

[27] A term popularized by the defense team of O.J. Simpson and used to acquit him.

Prostitution of Justice

[28] People v. Miller, 99CR2023, (District Court of Jefferson County, February 27, 2001).

[29] Deseret News, August 15, 1997.

[30] Christopher Anderson, "Reporter Suing Ramseys Over Book," Boulder Daily Camera, p. 1.

[31] John Douglas and Mark Olshaker, The Cases that Haunt Us (New York: A Lisa Drew Book/Scribner's, 2000), 332.

[32] Hodges, A Mother Gone Bad, pp. 231–232. [1] John Douglas and Mark Olshaker, The Cases That Haunt Us, Simon & Schuster, Inc., New York, 2000, p. 292.

[33] John Douglas and Mark Olshaker, The Cases That Haunt Us, Simon & Schuster, Inc., New York, 2000, p. 292.

[34] Douglas, p. 292.

[35] Andrew G. Hodges, A Mother Gone Bad, Village House Publishers, Birmingham AB, 1998, pg. 223.

[36] Thomas, JonBenet: Inside the Ramsey Murder Investigation, 311

[37] Alex Hunter, CBS, KCNC Denver, October 13, 1999.

[38] CNN, interview, January 1, 1997.

[39] Lawrence Schiller, Perfect Murder, Perfect Town (New York: Harper Collins Publishers, 1998),112. Craig Lewis provided author Larry Schiller with the details of how tabloid reporters would invade a city or town for a news story, hire all the private investigators, purchase information worth thousands of dollars, and "own" the information available within days, if not hours, calling it a "gang bang."

[40] Author's interview with Brett Sawyer, July 13, 2001.

[41] CNN, The Larry King Show, September 2, 1997.

[42] Ramsey and Ramsey, The Death of Innocence, 220.

[43] Sawyer interview, ibid.

Prostitution of Justice

[44] Alli Krupski, *The Boulder Daily Camera*, "Lab Worker: I Was Betrayed-Man charged in photo theft blames friend," January 19, 1997, Sec. A-1.

[45] Sawyer interview, ibid.

[46] Schiller, *Perfect Murder, Perfect Town*, 112.

[47] Sawyer interview, ibid.

[48] Sebastian, Matt, *Thomas Denies Paying Ramseys: Former Detective says he admitted no wrongdoing in settling libel case,* " Boulder Daily Camera, August 21, 2002. P. 3.

[49] Schiller, *Perfect Murder, Perfect Town*, 133–134.

[50] Author's interview with J.T. Colfax, August 2001.

[51] Harvey Steinberg had formerly worked as a prosecutor in the District Attorney's Office in Arapahoe County, Colorado. He embarrassed prosecutors in a jury trial acquittal of Bill Romanowski on drug charges. The DA in Arapahoe County dropped related accusations against the football player's wife.

For the Colorado Avalanche goalie, Patrick Roy, Harvey Steinberg convinced the DA that when the drunk and angry sports hero smashed in a door at his home, he could commit no act of domestic violence against a door, an inanimate object.

[52] Author's interview with J.T. Colfax, Ibid.

[53] Author's interview with J.T. Colfax, Ibid.

[54] Ibid.

[55] Schiller, *Perfect Murder, Perfect Town*, 123.

[56] Ramsey and Ramsey, *Death of Innocence*, 300.

[57] The author formerly owned Investigative Reporting Services, Inc.

[58] Ibid.

[59] Douglas Frantz, "Law Confronts Seller of Private Date," The New York Times, July 1, 1999,

[60] Financial Information Security Act of 1998: Hearings on H.R. 4321, Day 2, July 28, 1998, Before the Commerce Committee 105th Cong. (1998) (testimony of Al Schweitzer to amend the Consumer Protection Act.

[61] Schiller, Perfect Murder, Perfect Town, 160–162.

[62] Ramsey and Ramsey, Death of Innocence, 118.

[63] Schiller, Perfect Murder, Perfect Town, 158.

[64] Schiller, Perfect Murder, Perfect Town, 158–159.

[65] "Pasta Jay and the Law," Boulder Daily Camera, April 17, 1997. [Need the author and the page number.]

[66] https://www.msn.com/en-us/travel/news/more-americans-are-moving-to-tuscany-where-their-money-goes-further-the-pace-is-slower-and-the-wine-flows-freely/ar-BB1jdaxz

[67] Ramsey and Ramsey, Death of Innocence, 118.

[68] 10th Circuit Historical Society, "Oral History of Harold A. "Hal" Haddon" Esq., December 6-Decembr 7, 2020. The biographical and historical information of Mr. Haddon's life is provided from facts, statements, short phrases, names, words, and ideas restructured, taking only ideas from the 10th Circuit Historical Society's website.
http://www.10thusdisdtrictcourt.org/halhaddon

[69] "Oral History of Harold A. "Hal" Haddon, ibid.

[70] Duke Law Journal, F. Hodge O'Neal, Close Corporation Legislation: A Survey and an Evaluation, vol. 1962:867.
https://scholarship.law.duke.edu/cgi/viewcontent.cgi?article=2408&cont

ext=dlj.ttps://scholarship.law.duke.edu/cgi/viewcontent.cgi?article=2408&context=dlj.

[71] "Oral History of Harold A. "Hal" Haddon, ibid.

[72] 316 S.C. 455, (1942)

[73] "Oral History of Harold A. "Hal" Haddon, ibid.

[74] Oral History of Harold A. "Hal" Haddon, ibid.

[75] "Oral History of Harold A. "Hal" Haddon, ibid

[76] https://www.angelfire.com/me4/tmouse/rrogers.html.

[77] Oral History of Harold A. "Hal" Haddon, ibid.

[78] Albert Lieck, Journal of Criminal Law and Criminology, "Abolition of the Grand Jury in England," Volume 4, Issue, November-December, Article 10, https://scholarlycommonslaw.northwestern.edu/cgi/viewcontent.cgi?article=2501&context=jclc.

[79] People v. Miller, Jefferson County District Court, Case No. 00 CR 2023

Pretrial interview with Wally Barrett, Barrett & Associates, former Public Defenders Office Investigator,

Oral History of Harold A. "Hal" Haddon, ibid.

[80] This statute was dramatically revised following the 2001 trial in the Jefferson County District Court, Case No. 00 CR 2023, People of the State of Colorado v. Thomas C. Miller, in which the defendant (and author of this book) was acquitted in a three-day trial. The charges arose from Miller's location of the ransom note and a tabloid editor's (Craig A. Lewis) attempt to purchase it.

[81] Oral History of Harold A. "Hal" Haddon, ibid.

Prostitution of Justice

[82] O'Keeffe, Mike, Westword, "Look Who's Talking! When Jim Stone Blew the Whistle on Rocky Flats, the FBI came running, December 122-18, 1990, pg. 10.

[83] Westword, ibid.

[84] Westword, ibid.

[85] Barry Siegel, The Los Angeles Times, "Showdown at Rocky Flats: When Federal Agents Take on a Government Nuclear-Bomb Plant, Lines of Law and Politics Blur, and Moral Responsibility is Tested," August 8, 1993.

[86] Oral History of Harold A. "Hal" Haddon, ibid.

[87] Barry Siegel, The Los Angeles Times, "Showdown at Rocky Flats: When Federal Agents Take on a Government Nuclear-Bomb Plant, Lines of Law and Politics Blur, and Moral Responsibility is Tested," August 8, 1993.

[88] Letter from Fleet and Priscilla White: To the People of Colorado, Boulder Daily Camera, Pg. 1A, August 17, 1998.

Prostitution of Justice

Prostitution of Justice

Prostitution of Justice

www.ingramcontent.com/pod-product-compliance
Lightning Source LLC
Chambersburg PA
CBHW020454030426
42337CB00011B/108